(ANTI)EST.197

GATE
theatre

Gate Theatre presents

MEPHISTO
[A RHAPSODY]

By Samuel Gallet

Translated from the French by Chris Campbell

Adapted from the novel by Klaus Mann

Original text *Mephisto [Rhapsodie]*
by Samuel Gallet*

Directed by Kirsty Housley

CAST

Nicole	Subika Anwar-Khan
Aymeric Dupré	Leo Bill
Luca	Elizabeth Chan
Eva/Anna Bauer	Tamzin Griffin
Barbara	Rebecca Humphries
Théo Marber/Fabien Muller	Sean Jackson
Juliette Demba	Anna-Maria Nabirye
Michael	Rhys Rusbatch

CREATIVE TEAM

Writer	Samuel Gallet
Translator	Chris Campbell
Director	Kirsty Housley
Designer	Basia Bińkowska
Lighting Designer	Jessica Hung Han Yun
Sound Designers	Mike Winship
	Helen Skiera
Fight Director	Lisa Connell
Assistant Director	Kaleya Baxe
Assistant Designer	Amanda Ramasawmy
Production Manager	Tammy Rose
Stage Manager – on book	Devika Ramcharan
Stage Manager – props	Nina Harding
Production LX	Teresa Nagel
Production SFX	Will Thompson

The Gate would also like to thank the following people for their help with the development of this production: Jean Baptiste Pasquier, Jean Pierre Baro, Ben Hadley, Harlequin Floors, English Touring Theatre, Amin Ali, Barbara Smith, Catherine Chalk, Evangeline Cullingworth, Roberta Livingston and White Light.

CAST

SUBIKA ANWAR-KHAN
NICOLE
Subika studied Creative Writing and English Language at the University of Gloucestershire and has taken numerous performing arts training courses. Subika has previously appeared in *Julie* at the National Theatre, directed by Carrie Cracknell, and earlier this year secured her first television role as PC Nawaz across two episodes of BBC award winning soap *EastEnders*. Subika has recently finished filming *After Love,* a British feature film directed by BAFTA Nominated Aleem Khan, which secured her first feature film role.

LEO BILL
AYMERIC DUPRÉ
Theatre includes: *Dear Elizabeth* (Gate Theatre), *The Tragedy of King Richard The Second* (Almeida), *Curtains* (Rose Theatre), *A Midsummer Night's Dream, The Glass Menagerie* (Young Vic), *Hamlet* (The Barbican), *Light Shining in Buckinghamshire, A Woman Killed With Kindness, Pains of Youth, The Observer, The Hothouse, The Reporter* (National Theatre), *Posh* (Royal Court) and *Beautiful Thing* (Sound Theatre). Film includes: *Rare Beasts, In Fabric, Peterloo, Hamlet, Alice in Wonderland - Through The Looking Glass, Mr Turner, A Long Way Down, The Girl with the Dragon Tattoo, Me and Orson Wells, Becoming Jane, The Living and the Dead, Kinky Boots, These Foolish Things, The Fall, Vera Drake, LD50, Two Men Went To War, 28 Days Later, All or Nothing* and *Gosford Park.* TV includes: *The Long Song, The Strike Series, Taboo, The White Queen, Pramface, The Borgias, Words of Captain Scott, Dr Who - A Christmas Carol, Home Time, Ashes to Ashes, Lead Balloon, Sense and Sensibility, Jekyll, Bash, A Very Social Secretary, Silent Witness, Messiah III, Eroica, The Canterbury Tales, Spooks 2, Midsummer Murders, Harry Enfield's Celeb, Surrealismo, Attachments II* and *Crime and Punishment.*

ELIZABETH CHAN
LUCA
Elizabeth Chan trained at Ecole Philippe Gaulier in Paris and at Drama Centre London. Her work in theatre includes: *Dear Elizabeth* (Gate Theatre), *Shakespeare Walks* and *Shakespeare in the Abbey* (Shakespeare's Globe), *Macbeth, Light Shining in Buckinghamshire, Greenland* (National Theatre), *Celebration Florida* (Soho Theatre), *Henry IV* (Donmar Warehouse), *Chimerica* (Almeida/West End), *The Wheel* (National Theatre of Scotland), *Into the Numbers* (Finborough),

Birth (Royal Exchange), *The Sugar-Coated Bullets of the Bourgeoisie* (HighTide), *Caught, Hamlet is Dead* (Arcola), *Don't Shoot the Clowns* (Fuel), *An Argument About Sex* (Traverse/Tramway), *Cinderella* (Lyric Hammersmith). TV includes: *Vera, Chimerica, NoOffence, Motherland, Carters Get Rich, The Last Dragonslayer, Last Tango in Halifax, Cucumber, Holby City, Black Mirror* and Silent Witness. Television credits include: *Lawful Killing* (BBC One) and #*Hood Documentary* (BBC Three/ Fudge Park Productions). Short film credits include: *Pipe Up* (Company of Angels).

TAMZIN GRIFFIN
EVA/ANNA BAUER

Theatre includes: *Present Laughter, Tonight at 8:30* (Chichester Festival Theatre), *St George and the Dragon, Draw Me Close* (National Theatre/ Tribeca Film Festival/Young Vic), *Emil and the Detectives, Greenland and Our Class* (National Theatre), *The War Has Not Yet Started* (Theatre Royal Plymouth), *Cyrano de Bergerac* (Southwark Playhouse), *The Hudsucker Proxy* (Nuffield Theatre Southampton and Liverpool Everyman), *Far Away and Red Demon* (Young Vic), *Jedermann* (Salzburger Festspiele), *The Empress* and *Othello* (RSC), *The Master and Margarita* (Complicite/ Barbican & international tour), *A Dog's Heart* (Complicite/Opera House Amsterdam), *Brief Encounter* (Kneehigh/Birmingham Rep & Haymarket West End), *A Matter of Life and Death* (Kneehigh/National Theatre), *Rough Magyck* (Forkbeard Fantasy/RSC), *Measure for Measure* (Complicite/ National Theatre & international tour), *Red Demon* (Tokyu Bunkamura), *Strange Poetry* (Complicite/LA Philharmonic), *San Diego* (Tron and Edinburgh Festival), *Witness* (Gate Theatre and BAC), *Shockheaded Peter* (Lyric Hammersmith, West Yorkshire Playhouse, national and international tour: Olivier Award for Best Entertainment), *Nothing Lasts Forever* (BAC), *The Fear Show* (ICA), *The Lights Are On But Nobody's Home* (Royal Court Theatre), *Obituary* (ICA and Maubeuge International Festival France), *Demon Lovers* (Meeting Ground Theatre Company), *House* (Paines Plough/Salisbury Playhouse), *Ron Koop's Last Roadshow* (BBC/Industrial & Domestic), *Civic Monument* (Serpentine Gallery and tour). Television and film includes: *Dad's Army, Holby City, ABC Murders, Some Candid Observations on the Eve of the End of the World, A Fantastic Fear of Everything, Alice, Chernobyl: Surviving Disaster, Casualty, Casanova, The Calcium Kid, Smack the Pony, Doctors, Kabhi Khushi Kabhie Gham, Roadrunner, Rolf's Animal Hairdressers, Bob and Margaret, Teletubbies, Suburban Psycho, The Pay Off, Great Britain* and *Medus*. Radio includes: *Pericles, The Gestapo Minutes* and *The Fireraisers*.

REBECCA HUMPHRIES
BARBARA

Theatre credits include: *Myth and Earthworks* (RSC), *Wild Honey, The Argument* (Hampstead Theatre), *Pomona* (Orange Tree, then National Theatre), *The Kitchen* (National Theatre), *Temple* (Donmar Warehouse), *Open Court: Primetime* (Royal Court), *I Am A Camera* (Southwark Playhouse) and *24 Hour Plays* (Old Vic). As a writer, director and performer: *Prom Kween* (Udderbelly, Cowgate) and *Dizney Rascal* (Otherplace). TV credits include: *Trigonometry, The Agency, Cockroaches, Big Bad World, Sean Walsh World, Come Fly With Me* and *Cardinal Burns*. Radio credits include: *The World According to Harry Priest* and *Riot Girls*.

SEAN JACKSON
THÉO MARBER/FABIEN MULLER

Theatre includes: *Eden* (Hampstead Theatre), *Mrs Dalloway* (Arcola Theatre), *Macbeth* (Shrewsbury), *The Hook* (Northampton/Liverpool Everyman), *Antony & Cleopatra, Holy Warriors* (Shakespeare's Globe), *Richard III* (Nottingham Playhouse/York Theatre Royal), *Say It With Flowers* (Hampstead), *Beauty and the Beast, Waves* (also New York), *The Seagull, A Dream Play, The Mandate, Iphigenia at Aulis, The Talking Cure, Ivanov* (National Theatre), *Richard II, Hamlet* (also Broadway), *The Wild Duck* (Donmar), *The Jewish Wife* (Young Vic) and *Henry V* (Manchester Royal Exchange). TV and film includes: *The Innocents, Eddie the Eagle, Da Vinci's Demons* (2 series), *The Fear, Silent Witness, Waking the Dead, Eastenders* and *No Man's Land*. Audio includes: *Dalek Empire 3 - The Exterminators* and *Doctor Who - The Marian Conspiracy* (Big Finish).

ANNA-MARIA NABIRYE
JULIETTE DEMBA

Anna-Maria Nabirye played Macduff earlier this year in the Sam Wanamaker Playhouse's *Macbeth*. Other theatre credits include: *We Know Not What We May Be* (Metis Theatre/The Barbican), *The Paper Man*, (Improbable Theatre), *Macbeth & Les Blancs* (National Theatre), *Boudica & A Midsummer Night's Dream* (Shakespeare's Globe), *They Drink It In The Congo* (Almeida), *Richard III, Medea, Blood Wedding, Fiesco, Three Sisters* (The Faction), *Egusi Soup* (Menagerie Theatre & Theatre Royal Bury St. Edmunds), *Leaving Planet Earth* (Grid Iron), *24 HOUR PLAYS* (Old Vic), *Mad Blud* (Theatre Royal Stratford East), *Ugly* (Reddladder) and *Handa's Hen* (Little Angel Theatre). Television credits include: *Elizabeth Is Missing* (BBC1), *Informer* (BBC1), *Collateral* (BBC2), *Waterloo Road* (BBC) and *Misfits* (E4). Film credits include: *The Scar* (Film London), *The Keeping Room* (Gilbert Films) and *The Briny* (DNA/Film4). Anna-Maria creates, writes and directs her own live art, theatre and film. Her current works are: *Up In Arms*, currently supported by Arts Admin, and *Motherhoody,* a commission from The Albany supported by Arts Council England.

RHYS RUSBATCH
MICHAEL

Rhys trained at The Guildhall School of Music and Drama. Theatre includes: *Knives In Hens* (Perth Theatre), *The Rivals* (Bristol Old Vic/ Citizens), *Wendy and Peter Pan* (RSC), *Mametz, The Persians* (National Theatre of Wales), *Hannah, Not Now Bernard, Henry V* (Unicorn Theatre/Tour), *A Midsummer Night's Dream* (Lyric, Hammersmith/ Royal Exchange/ UK Tour), *Greenland, Our Class* (National Theatre), *Eurydice* (Young Vic) and *Sitcom Trials* (Leicester Square). TV includes: *Sherlock, Merlin* and *In Search of Pete Doherty*. Film includes: *Dirt Ash Meat, Burn Burn Burn, Zero Dark Thirty* and *Hunky Dory*. Radio: *Ed Reardon*.

CREATIVE TEAM

SAMUEL GALLET
WRITER

Born in 1981, Samuel Gallet is a playwright and poet – he regularly adapts his dramatic poems for the stage with a company of musicians. The majority of his work has been produced in France and internationally as well as being broadcast on France Culture Radio. He runs the Eskander collective and is co-director of the department of writing and dramaturgy at the Ensatt. Among his work, which has been published by Editions Espaces 34, are the following plays: *Autopsie du Gibier* (in the collection Le Monde Me Tue), *Encore un Jour Sans, Communiqué n°10* (2011), *Oswald de Nuit*, a trilogy including *Oswald, L'Ennemi* and *Rosa*, (2012), *Issues* (2015), *La Bataille d'Eskandar* (2017), *La Ville Ouverte* (2018) and *Mephisto Rhapsodie* (2019).

CHRIS CAMPBELL
TRANSLATOR

Chris is the Editorial Director of Oberon Books. He was previously Literary Manager of the Royal Court Theatre and, before that, for six years, he was Deputy Literary Manager of the National Theatre. He has translated plays by Philippe Minyana, David Lescot, Rémi de Vos, Adeline Picault, Magali Mougel, Launcelot Hamelin, Frédéric Blanchette, Catherine-Anne Toupin and Fabrice Roger-Lacan for the National Theatre, the Gate Theatre, the Almeida, the Donmar Warehouse, the Traverse and the Young Vic among others. In 2017, Oberon Books published a collection of his contemporary French translations. Recent productions include *Right Now* (Traverse/Bush/Ustinov) and *Suzy Storck* (Gate Theatre). As an actor Chris has worked at theatres including the National Theatre, the Royal Court, the Traverse, the West Yorkshire Playhouse, the Birmingham Rep, the Gate and English Touring Theatre.

Directors have included Howard Davies, Sir Richard Eyre, Sir Peter Hall, Richard Wilson, William Gaskill, Erica Whyman, Stephen Daldry, Ian Brown and Annie Castledine. Most recently, he appeared alongside Meryl Streep in *The Iron Lady*. In 2013 he was appointed Chevalier de l'Ordre des Arts et Lettres by the French government.

KIRSTY HOUSLEY
DIRECTOR

Current and future credits include: *Avalanche* (Barbican - dramaturg), *Tao of Glass* (Manchester International Festival) and *Rich Kids: A History of Shopping Malls in Tehran* (Traverse - co-creator). Theatre works include: *I'm a Phoenix, Bitch* (Battersea Arts Centre, touring - co-director), *Grimm Tales* (Unicorn), *The Distance* (Roundhouse), *Misty* (Bush Theatre/ West End - dramaturg), *The Believers Are But Brothers* (Bush Theatre, Ovalhouse, West Yorkshire Playhouse Transform17 season and Northern Stage Edinburgh – co-director), *Myth* (RSC – co-written with Matt Hartley), *The Encounter* (Complicité, EIF, Warwick Arts Centre, Theatre Vidy, Bristol Old Vic, UK tour - co-director), *A Pacifist's Guide to the War on Cancer* (dramaturg, National Theatre and Complicité, director – international tour), *Wanted* (Chris Goode and Company, Transform Festival, West Yorkshire Playhouse), *Walking the Tightrope* (Offstage and Theatre Uncut), *All I Want* (Live Theatre, Leeds Libraries and Jackson's Lane), *Mass* (Amy Mason at Bristol Old Vic, Camden People's Theatre), *The Beauty Project*, Theatre Uncut 2012 (Young Vic), *How to Be Mortal* (Penny Dreadful at Soho and tour), *Bandages* (Corn Exchange Newbury and tour), *9* (West Yorkshire Playhouse for Chris Goode and Company) and *Thirsty* (The Paper Birds). Kirsty has been the recipient of the Oxford Samuel Beckett Theatre Trust Award and the Title Pending award for innovation at Northern Stage. She is an associate of Complicité and working with a number of independent artists.

BASIA BIŃKOWSKA
DESIGNER

Basia is a performance designer based in London. Before completing a theatre design course in the UK, she trained in fine arts in her native Poland. She is the overall winner of the Linbury Prize for Stage Design 2017 with the winning design for the Lyric Hammersmith's production of *Othellomacbeth*. She was nominated for Best Designer at the Stage Debut Awards 2018 and has been recently nominated for an Offie for Best Set Design for *Blood Knot* at the Orange Tree. Recent credits include: *Crooked Dances* (Royal Shakespeare Company), *Acts of Resistance* (Headlong Theatre & Bristol Old Vic), *Wolfie* (Theatre503), *Blood Knot* (Orange Tree Theatre), *Othellomacbeth* (Lyric Hammersmith & Home Manchester), *Cuckoo* (Soho Theatre), *Devil with a Blue Dress* (Bunker Theatre) and most recently, *Ivan and the Dogs* (Young Vic).

JESSICA HUNG HAN YUN
LIGHTING DESIGNER

Credits include: *EQUUS* (ETT), *Pah-la* (Royal Court), *Armadillo* (The Yard), *Seven Methods of Killing Kylie Jenner* (Royal Court), *The Human Voice* (Gate Theatre), *Cuckoo* (Metal Rabbit Productions), *Snowflake* (Arts Old Fire Station), *One* (Bert & Nasi International Tour), *Forgotten* (Yellow Earth & Moongate UK Tour), *Dear Elizabeth* (Gate Theatre), *Into The Clouds* (Nonsuch Theatre Company International Tour), *Hive City Legacy* (Hot Brown Honey & Roundhouse), *The Party's Over* (Nonsuch Theatre Company), *Gypsy Disco* (Boomtown Festival), *Becoming Shades* (Chivaree Circus) and *Nine Foot Nine* (Sleepless Theatre Company).

MIKE WINSHIP
SOUND DESIGNER

Recent sound designs include: *Youth Without God* (Coronet), *#HonestAmy* (Pleasance, Edinburgh), *Sonny* (ArtsEd), *Anatomy of a Suicide* (Central School of Speech & Drama), *Anna X* (Vault Festival), *The Jumper Factory* (Young Vic), *The Winter's Tale* (National Theatre & Schools Tour), *The Mysteries* (Manchester Royal Exchange), *The Human Voice* (Gate Theatre), *Zoo* (Theatre503) and *Shadows (Eurydice Speaks)* (Schaubühne, Berlin). As Associate Sound Designer: *Macbeth, Hedda Gabler* (National Theatre, UK & Ireland Tours), *The Girl on the Train* (West End / UK & Ireland Tour) and *The Hairy Ape* (Park Avenue Armory, New York). Other sound work includes: Sound design for Bastille's *Doom Days* Amazon Music album launch campaign, Binaural sound recordist for Opera North's *Aeons* sound walk, as part of the Great Exhibition of the North 2018 and Assistant sound designer on Land Rover's binaural *Discovery Adventures* podcast.

HELEN SKIERA
SOUND DESIGNER

Credits include: *Out Of Water* (Orange Tree), *A Christmas Carol* (Bristol Old Vic), *The Lovely Bones* (Royal and Derngate and Tour), *This Is Not For You* (Graeae GDIF and SIRF), *Instructions For Correct Assembly, Bodies* (Royal Court Theatre), *Imber* (You Walk Through), *Betrayal, Echo's End, The Magna Carta Plays* (Salisbury Playhouse), *The Encounter* (Complicite), *Crossings, Here I belong* (Pentabus), *Good Dog, I Know All The Secrets In My World, The Epic Adventure of Nhamo The Manyika Warrior and his Sexy Wife Chipo, The Legend of Hamba* (Tiata Fahodzi), *House and Garden* (Watermill), *Harajuku Girls* (Finborough Theatre), *The Dog, The Night, and The Knife, Pandora's Box, Sister Of, Miss Julie* (Arcola), *The Boy Who Climbed Out of His Face* (Shunt), *The Last Words You'll Hear* (Almeida at Latitude), *Advice for the Young at Heart* (Theatre Centre), *The Centre* (Islington Community Theatre), *The Three Sisters,*

The Laramie Project, (GSMD), *Snow White, US/UK Exchange* (Old Vic New Voices), *Meat* (Bush Theatre). As Associate: *Barbershop Chronicles* (National Theatre), *Cat on a Hot Tin Roof* (Young Vic/West End), *Adler and Gibb* (Royal Court Theatre) and *I'd Rather Goya Robbed Me of My Sleep Than Some Other Arsehole* (The Gate).

LISA CONNELL
FIGHT DIRECTOR

Lisa Connell is an APC qualified Stage Combat instructor, fight choreographer and Action Performer. She is a resident Stage Combat Teacher at PPA in Guildford and Northampton University. Recent Fight Direction includes: *The Scarlet Pimpernel* (Everyman Theatre Cheltenham), *Approaching Empty* (Kiln Theatre), *Heathers: The Musical* (Theatre Royal Haymarket, The Other Palace), *Comedy of Errors* and *Julius Caesar* (RSC - First Encounters Tours). She is currently in rehearsals with The Welsh National Opera for Bizet's *Carmen*.

KALEYA BAXE
ASSISTANT DIRECTOR

Kaleya Baxe is a writer, director and facilitator who studied Drama, Applied Theatre and Education BA (Hons) at the Royal Central School of Speech and Drama. Previously, she has directed *Patricia Gets Ready* (White Bear Theatre), *Deux Femme on the Edge de la Revolution* (short, Roundhouse) and *Wine Down* (short, Theatre503). She has previously assisted on *Radio* (Arcola Theatre) and is currently training on the Young Vic's Intro to Directing programme, mentored by Roy Alexander Weise. Kaleya is also a recipient of the MGCFutures Assistant Director Bursary 2019. Her debut play *Never Forget* was recently staged at the Tristan Bates Theatre, John Thaw Studio as part of the Blacktress season.

AMANDA RAMASAWMY
ASSISTANT DESIGNER

Amanda is a scenographer and artist from London, working across performance design, installation and moving image mediums. She graduated from the Royal Central School of Speech and Drama in 2018 with a Masters in Scenography. Previous to that she worked in film production design. She is currently part of Constellations, an artist residency focussed on exploring social-political issues, collaboration and activating public spaces. She's most interested in finding non-traditional ways to communicate stories, particularly those from marginalised communities that are yet to be told.

TAMMY ROSE
PRODUCTION MANAGER

DEVIKA RAMCHARAN
STAGE MANAGER – BOOK
Devika is a Stage Manager in London and holds a BA in Theatre Practice: Stage Management from the Royal Central School of Speech and Drama. Credits as SM on Book include: *Blue Door* (Ustinov at TRB), *Kettle of Fish* (The Yard) and *Ali and Dahlia* (The Pleasance). As DSM: *Can't Wait for Christmas!* (Orange Tree) and *Aladdin* (Oxford Playhouse). As ASM: *Wake* (Birmingham Opera), *Pity* (Royal Court), *Another World* (NT), *Les Miserables* (Pimlico Opera) and *The Mother* (Tricycle).

NINA HARDING
STAGE MANAGER – PROPS
Nina studied Theatre: Writing, Directing and Performance at the University of York. Since graduating in 2017, she has worked as a Stage Manager in London. Stage Manager – Props credits include: *A Small Place* (Gate Theatre). As Technical Assistant Stage: *Cinderella* (The New Victoria Theatre) and *Home Sweet Home* (Tour). As Assistant Stage Manager: *Dido* (Unicorn Theatre) and *Dear Elizabeth* (Gate Theatre). As Stage Manager on the Book: *Stripped* (The Kings Head Theatre), *Catherine and Anita* (The King's Head Theatre), *Yokes Night* (Theatre Royal Stratford East) and *The Melting Pot* (Finborough Theatre).

TERESA NAGEL
PRODUCTION LX

WILL THOMPSON
PRODUCTION SFX
Will is a London based sound designer, composer and production engineer for theatre and performance and a graduate of the Royal Central School of Speech and Drama. Production credits include: *Either* (Hampstead Theatre), *Showstopper! - the improvised musical* (Tour and West End), *Cruel Intentions* (Edinburgh Fringe), *Peter Pan* (Park200), various at Shakespeare Rose Theatre, York and *Skate Hard Turn Left* (Battersea Arts Centre). Design credits include: *Salome* (Lazarus Theatre, Greenwich), *Into The Unknown* (Pentabus, Courtyard Theatre), *J'ouvert* (Theatre503), *The Gulf* (Mitchel Green Productions, Tristan Bates), *Jack and the Beanstalk* (Spillers, Epsom Playhouse), *Maggot Moon* (The Unicorn), *Telescope* (Aloff Theatre, Testbed1), *The Gambit* (Rampant Plays, The Edinburgh Festival Fringe) and *All In The Timing* (Chubbyhumm, The Edinburgh Festival Fringe).

ABOUT THE GATE THEATRE

(ANTI)EST.1979

GATE
theatre

'London's most relentlessly ambitious theatre'
Time Out

The Gate Theatre was founded in 1979 to present ground-breaking international plays to a London audience.

Today, the Gate exists to make international theatre that asks essential questions about ourselves, each other and the world. Our work investigates what it means to be alive now.

We imagine our work as a live conversation with our audience. Everyone is welcome in our intimate 75 seat theatre. Our space transforms with every production – no two visits are ever the same.

We nurture the best and most diverse new talent to push the boundaries of what theatre is and what else it could be. We create space for radical, inventive thinking to surprise, delight, challenge and inspire.

Our mission and our approach to delivering it strives to embody our organisational values of community, diversity, invention, internationalism and sustainability.

The Gate Theatre Company is a company limited by guarantee.
Registered in England & Wales No. 1495543 I Charity No. 280278
Registered address: 11 Pembridge Road, Above the Prince Albert Pub, London, W11 3HQ

Supported using public funding by
ARTS COUNCIL ENGLAND
LOTTERY FUNDED

(ANTI)EST.1979

GATE
theatre

Each year, the Gate needs to raise over £280,000 in philanthropic support in order to keep taking challenging artistic risks whilst keeping ticket prices low and affordable for all. Our Supporters play a very real and important part in helping us to continue to nurture and support emerging international artists whilst ensuring that their work is made accessible to wide and diverse audiences, and expanding our vital community work.

Our Supporters sit right at the heart of the Gate and are invited behind the scenes to discover more about our productions and meet our exciting artists, the theatre leaders of tomorrow.

Please join and help us continue to grow our activities and support the most exceptional new talent.

To make a gift or join as a Gate Supporter, please contact
development@gatetheatre.co.uk
020 7229 5387
www.gatetheatre.co.uk

The Gate Theatre is a registered charity (No. 280278).

The Gate Theatre's 40th anniversary season is supported by Cockayne – Grants for the Arts and the London Community Foundation.

We are grateful to the following individuals and Trusts and Foundations for their support of the Gate's work.

SPECIAL THANKS TO
David and Jean Grier and Addy Loudiadis.

GATE PIONEERS AND GUARDIANS
Kate Maltby, Charles and Barbara Prideaux, Linda and David Lakhdhir.

GATE AMBASSADORS
Eva Boenders and Scott Stevens, David Lacey, Kirsty and Iona Luke, David and Susie Sainsbury, Jon and NoraLee Sedmak and Sandi and Jake Ulrich.

GATE KEEPERS
The Agency (London) Ltd., Bruno and Christiane Boesch, Ariane Braillard and Francesco Cincotta, Dr Geraldine Brodie, Sarah and Phillippe Chappatte, Charles Cormick, Robert Devereux, Charles Glanville and James Hogan, Richard and Jan Grandison, Anatol Orient and Stephanie and Aaron Pottruck Goldman.

Thank you to all our Gate Openers and other supporters, and those who wish to remain anonymous.

TRUSTS AND FOUNDATIONS
Arts Council England, Jerwood Arts, Backstage Trust, the Royal Borough of Kensington and Chelsea, the Goethe-Institut, Cockayne – Grants for the Arts, the London Community Foundation, Ernest Hecht Charitable Foundation and National Lottery Awards for All.

CORPORATE SUPPORTERS
Douglas & Gordon

JERWOOD DESIGNERS AT THE GATE

Since 2001, the Jerwood Designers Programme has given outstanding designers and design assistants in the early stages of their careers the unique opportunity to design a full production at the Gate Theatre whilst developing their experience and expertise.

This partnership is an essential part of the Gate's identity as a theatre - enabling us to offer designers the opportunity to completely re-imagine how our space is configured for every show. Alumni of the programme include Chloe Lamford, Jon Bausor, Fly Davis, Soutra Gilmour, Tom Scutt and Rosie Elnile.

"Ground-breaking and visionary design is a key part of the Gate Theatre's identity. This reputation has been built on the generous support of Jerwood Arts and we are hugely grateful for it."

Ellen McDougall, Artistic Director

Jerwood Arts is the leading independent funder dedicated to supporting UK artists, curators and producers to develop and thrive. We enable transformative opportunities for individuals across art forms, supporting imaginative awards, bursaries, fellowships, projects, programmes and commissions. We present new work and bring people from across the arts together through our exhibitions and events in London, as well as across the UK. www.jerwoodarts.org

GREEN GATE

We want to imagine a different, better future with everyone who comes through our doors.

At the Gate Theatre, we recognise that we have a vital part to play in changing attitudes and approaches to environmental sustainability and climate change. We tell stories that help us question and imagine who we are as individuals and as communities, our social responsibility, and our future. We are passionate about ensuring that our programming is underpinned by recognition of this responsibility. The Gate was founded in 1979 to present ground-breaking international work, and so the narrative around climate change is intrinsic to the work we make and how we run our organisation: global equality, conflict and the natural world are inextricably linked, and an essential component of a theatre with an international outlook.

"The climate crisis is also a crisis of the imagination. If we cannot imagine a more sustainable and just way of living we cannot achieve it. Artistic and cultural institutions can be powerhouses of change, helping to create and forge new ways of thinking and doing. Now is the time to meet the emergency with imagination."

Anthony Simpson-Pike, Associate Artist

We are very happy to report that we have been awarded 4 stars from Julie's Bicycle Creative Green Assessment for our actions and efforts in making sustainable theatre.

Creative Green is a certification from Julie's Bicycle which provides organisations with a systematic, achievable and inspiring approach to environmental sustainability. It celebrates environmental success and shines a light on areas for improvement and gives your organisation a star rating from 1 to 5.

A MANIFESTO FOR OUR FUTURE

PROCESS IS POLITICAL

It is relevant who makes the work.
Amplify the voices silenced by the canon.
Text is not the only form of authorship.
Our artists are international.
Our shows are multilingual.
Our rehearsals are open.

FORM IS POLITICAL

Look outside what you know.
Rethink definitions of excellence.
Celebrate subjectivity.
Celebrate the mess and imperfection of humanity.
Celebrate liveness.

OUR WORK IS PART OF THE WORLD

Acknowledge and hold the suffering of the past.
Imagine the future.
Don't portray the world, change it.
We are nature and nature is us.
There must be space to come together and talk.
We declare a climate emergency.

CHANGE. TRANSITION. TRANSFORM.

Make work in a circular economy (and only 20% of materials can be new).
The shows (and all the conversations too) must leave the building.
Texts from earlier than 2010 must be radically interrogated.
At least one show in every season must be made outside the UK.
Everyone in the room is part of the show (this includes the audience).
We can't do this without you.
What happens after the play is the point of the play.

MEPHISTO [A RHAPSODY]

Samuel Gallet

MEPHISTO [A RHAPSODY]

Translated from the French by Chris Campbell

Adapted from the novel by Klaus Mann

Original text *Mephisto [Rhapsodie]* by Samuel Gallet

OBERON BOOKS
LONDON

WWW.OBERONBOOKS.COM

First published in the English language in 2019 by Oberon Books Ltd
521 Caledonian Road, London N7 9RH
Tel: +44 (0) 20 7607 3637 / Fax: +44 (0) 20 7607 3629
e-mail: info@oberonbooks.com
www.oberonbooks.com

PB ISBN: 9781786829535
E ISBN: 9781786829542

Cover image: Rosie Elnile / Emma Digby

10 9 8 7 6 5 4 3 2 1

Characters

AYMERIC DUPRÉ, 33, acting company member with the Balbek Theatre.

LUCA, 27, acting company member with the Balbek Theatre

NICOLE, 23, acting company member with the Balbek Theatre

MICHAEL, 21, trainee actor, sympathiser with the Front Line movement.

EVA, 50, Artistic Director of the Balbek Theatre.

BARBARA, 23, daughter of Anna Bauer

ANNA BAUER, 50, Director of the New Theatre

JULIETTETE DEMBA, 30, popular singer and actress

THÉO MARBER, 55, feared theatre critic

FABIEN MÜLLER, 50, MP, populist leader, founder of the Front Line movement

KLAUS MANN, German writer, author of *Mephisto*

ERIKA MANN, German actress, sister of Klaus Mann

RICHARD STRAUSS, German composer and conductor

WILHELM FURTWÄNGLER, German composer and conductor

GOTTFRIED BENN, expressionist poet

A BUTLER

PART ONE

A LONG WAY FROM THE BIG CITY

LUCA: When I was a student

We had this political science teacher

He'd come in

And take his lessons

And there was the odd time

When we were doing the history of twentieth-century revolutions

He'd go quiet

And we'd just sit there

And after a long pause

He'd say

With a note of embarrassment

'They expect a lot from us

People always had hope for those who would come after them

All those people who failed, well they're watching us now

And hoping we won't let it all slide back into darkness this time.'

For a long time I felt that gaze on me like a weight of guilt

All the dead there watching me

Those who'd fought

And been destroyed by the Leviathan

They were watching me and it felt like I was being found wanting

Judged in the dock

And I used to think

I can't do this

And I was ashamed

But then we learned to live together

The dead and me

They were still there

But they stopped judging me

They urged me gently on

Sometimes whispering in my ear not to give up

And I tried again and again not to disappoint their expectations

And to keep the possibility of a different kind of history alive

And he's always there in my memory, ageless, in a corner, in his chair

Saying nothing

Embarrassed

Just sometimes raising his head

To mumble

'If the enemy triumphs even the dead won't be safe'

1.

Balbek, a small provincial town somewhere out in the regions.

A theatre. In the theatre bar, EVA, AYMERIC and LUCA drinking.

Off to one side, MICHAEL looks out into the night.

Enthusiastic applause off.

AYMERIC: Four bows.

EVA: It's all rubbish.

AYMERIC: I'm jealous.

EVA: No one comes to see anything good anymore.

AYMERIC: I want a pay rise.

EVA: We have to cast names.

AYMERIC: I can't stand these provincial holes.

EVA: People only care about fame, power and money.

AYMERIC: I don't blame them.

EVA: I was at a meeting with Juliettete Demba yesterday. She was giving a talk. Doing the deep and serious voice she goes, 'Theatre. There is only the theatre. Everything for the theatre.' And everyone thought it was just great.

AYMERIC: Theatre. There is only the theatre. Everything for the theatre.

EVA: Yes, it doesn't work when *you* say it. How can I give you a pay rise?

AYMERIC: Fifth bow.

EVA: Stick a star name in it and they come swarming in like flies.

LUCA: It is possible to be famous *and* talented surely?

AYMERIC: I want to be paid like Juliettete Demba.

EVA: Does your name sell tickets? And I'm not talking about your unemployed mates from drama school who can barely keep their heads above water.

LUCA: I really like Juliettete Demba. Her voice, her presence.

MICHAEL: She's a foreigner.

LUCA: She's great.

MICHAEL: Just because she's black.

EVA: Michael, please don't start on that again.

Exit MICHAEL.

The show comes down. Lots of people. The audience spilling out of the theatre.

JULIETTEte DEMBA enters.

JULIETTETE: Darlings! Hello!

EVA: Juliettete, will you have a drink with us?

JULIETTETE: I have to go, I have a date.

AYMERIC: I'm sorry Juliettete, but I simply can't let you go until I tell you how very much I appreciate your work.

JULIETTETE: You weren't in, Aymeric.

AYMERIC: Excuse me?

JULIETTETE: You didn't see the show.

AYMERIC: I was in the front row. I couldn't take my eyes off you.

JULIETTETE: And now he's lying to my face. He lies like it's true.

AYMERIC: You were fantastic tonight, Juliette. I know that. Sometimes I'd like to be the only person doing theatre. All the people who make up the theatre, all the other actors, all the other actresses, I wish they'd all just die, disappear from the face of the earth and leave me centre stage in the spotlight on my own. Do you know what I mean?

JULIETTETE: Of course. I think all actors have that. See you later.

She exits.

AYMERIC goes back to his seat, slumping next to EVA.

AYMERIC: We'll never be famous if we stay in this hole.

LUCA: We'll never be famous if we stay doing theatre.

EVA: We're going to have to do something else, aren't we?

LUCA: Political theatre, Eva.

EVA: Preaching to people who already agree with you?

LUCA: We have to warn against the rise of fascism. Because fascism is coming back. Oh yes, it's back in Europe.

EVA: I don't think you can call it fascism.

LUCA: Sometimes I wonder what world you live in.

EVA: I'd ask you the same question.

Enter NICOLE.

Followed by BARBARA with a travel bag.

NICOLE: Hi all.

BARBARA: Hello.

NICOLE: This is Barbara. My lovely friend. Barbara, this is the Balbek Theatre family.

AYMERIC: We are the Balbek theatre family.

EVA: How was the journey?

BARBARA: Long. The train was two hours late.

NICOLE: We hit a wild boar!

BARBARA: I thought I'd be in time for Juliettete Demba.

EVA: Public transport in the regions. And now they want to cut the line. You want to kill off a region, you cut the transport links and you get the desired result very quickly. Can I get you something? How about a beer? Wine?

BARBARA: A beer, thank you.

EVA takes BARBARA to the bar.

AYMERIC: Who is that?

NICOLE: Anna Bauer's daughter.

LUCA: Who?

AYMERIC: Anna Bauer. Artistic Director of the New Theatre.

BARBARA and EVA come back and sit down.

BARBARA: I wanted to know if I could sit in on your rehearsals?

EVA: No problem at all.

AYMERIC: Do you know Chekhov?

BARBARA: Not very well.

LUCA: What about Ernst Toller?

EVA: We're not changing the play, Luca.

LUCA: Everyone does Chekhov.

EVA: There's a reason for that.

NICOLE: Did you see what happened in that refugee camp?

LUCA: What?

NICOLE: A dozen extreme-right bastards stormed into the camp in hoodies, throwing smoke bombs. They hit the men with baseball bats. Gassed women and children. Set fire to tents. About 30 people injured.

LUCA: What was I saying, Eva?

NICOLE: Someone filmed and shared.

They watch the clip on NICOLE's phone.

Pause.

EVA: How awful.

BARBARA: And it's not the first time.

LUCA: We have to dump the Chekhov.

EVA: What? Why?

LUCA: We can't just do another bloody *Cherry Orchard*.

EVA: I'm tired of this, Luca. Honestly, get yourself organised. Make some appointments. Raise some money from somewhere.

LUCA: We'll reach out to the communities where the fascists get most votes. I've made a mash-up version of the text. We'll read you an extract tomorrow.

EVA: And what? We all kiss at the end of the show, have a nice big cry and sing 'The Internationale'? You seem to be stuck somewhere in the twentieth century.

LUCA: They're having some ridiculous 'save the white race' demo next week, the extreme right's getting more and more support in the polls.

Eva, I get up every morning. And I tell myself I just can't do it. I look around at people. Closed faces. Sealed off. The people sleeping on the street. Exponentially rising poverty. Nationalism. And I feel crushed under the weight of doing nothing. I feel like I'm living inside a fire. In a fireproof padded room. With a big space suit on. Watching the flames tear through the planet. And I tell myself I can't do it. That's all I'm saying, Eva. I don't think I deserve your sarcasm.

He exits.

NICOLE: It's all about the crazy love with Luca.

EVA: She's having trouble with her part.

BARBARA: Why are you looking at me like that?

AYMERIC: I feel like I've seen you somewhere before.

BARBARA: Oh here we go!

AYMERIC: Is that possible?

BARBARA: I have a pretty generic face.

AYMERIC: Do you want me to show you around the theatre?

BARBARA: Sure.

Exit AYMERIC and BARBARA.

2.

EVA: When Aymeric reads the theatre press, he's in agony

When he reads reviews

He's in agony

When he gets the season brochures from theatres

He's in agony

Any time he reads a name and it's not his

He's in agony

When he hears a compliment about someone else,

Agony

When someone's successful

Or very successful

Much more successful than he is, let's say

It gives him a migraine

He can't sleep

He's an actor in a theatre in a regional town

In Balbek

But the thought of fame

Real fame

Fame in the capital

That thought gnaws away at him like a physical disease

He thinks up schemes

Keeps up to date

Memorises the names of the men and women who pull the strings

In this little world he dreams of ruling over

Where he dreams of fierce revenge

He takes the train a lot

Never truly doubting

That the world in one way or another

Revolves around him

And that his day will come

He's an actor

He puts himself about

90% of his time is parties

Dates

Affairs

The other 10% he's on stage working

He can live with the times

The rise of extremes

Corruption

Mass unemployment

Turbo-capitalism

Men and women dying at border crossings

You can't stop Niagara Falls with an umbrella?

He can live with it.

We're in the first half of the 21st century

No one knows where they stand anymore

Things are always more complex

You have to howl with the wolves occasionally, so he howls

He's a man wading through the swamp of the times he lives in

He's just an actor.

He dreams of the bright lights

Of being talked about

Of being famous

Saved

Protected

By glory.

3.

Night, on the stage of the Balbek Theatre.

AYMERIC: There you go. This is where I live my life. Sometimes it's the only thing that's real. Two chairs on an empty stage.

BARBARA: I like the theatre. I mean, I go. I've been kind of interested since I was a little girl. I really envy you actors. You have a real passion. I can't get excited about anything. I'm kind of interested in loads, but nothing really grabs me.

AYMERIC: Being an actor. Just doing theatre. It's not enough today.

BARBARA: I don't understand.

AYMERIC: The political situation. What we don't do. What theatre can do.

BARBARA: Can it do anything though?

AYMERIC: We should try.

BARBARA: I don't really think the far right will get into power.

AYMERIC: People have been saying that for years and yet they're still on the rise. If the Front Line get elected, I'm giving up theatre and I'll be out fighting in the streets.

BARBARA: I hope that won't be necessary.

AYMERIC: We're at the mercy of thickos.

You have to live here in Balbek to know.

BARBARA: And where are you going to do the Chekhov?

AYMERIC: I'm going to get a meeting with Anna Bauer.

BARBARA: Oh, yes.

AYMERIC: She runs the New Theatre. Why are you laughing?

BARBARA: As if you didn't know.

AYMERIC: I don't understand.

BARBARA: She's my mother.

AYMERIC: Your mother? No, I didn't know that.

BARBARA: Right. Well, anyway.

AYMERIC: Everyone knows her.

BARBARA: What about you?

AYMERIC: I've read all her stuff.

BARBARA: What's your favourite?

AYMERIC: It's on the tip of my tongue.

BARBARA: *Barbaria*

AYMERIC: *Barbaria*, that's it!

BARBARA: It's so beautiful.

AYMERIC: And how long do you plan to stay here?

BARBARA: I don't know yet.

AYMERIC: At least until the opening night?

BARBARA: I hope so.

AYMERIC: It's going to be amazing.

BARBARA walks around on the stage.

BARBARA: Do you think I could take a look backstage?

AYMERIC: Of course.

She disappears backstage.

NICOLE comes in.

NICOLE: Do you fancy her?

AYMERIC: I'm not sure.

NICOLE: That's a good sign, right?

AYMERIC: I'm not sure where to start.

NICOLE: Start?

AYMERIC: With her body.

NICOLE: Like all of them.

AYMERIC: Where to touch it?

NICOLE: Are you going to have her?

BARBARA comes back with a little guitar.

BARBARA: Why are you looking at me like that?

NICOLE: We were just slagging you off, Barbara. You're glowing.

BARBARA: You're such an idiot.

She strums the guitar.

NICOLE: We're going to Barbara's mother's house this weekend. Then Monday to that camp that was attacked.

BARBARA: Do you want to come Aymeric?

AYMERIC: Yes, of course. You can't just stand back from this stuff.

NICOLE: Plus you can meet her mother.

BARBARA: And Juliettete Demba, she's my mother's partner.

NICOLE: It's down by the sea, about an hour's drive.

AYMERIC: Just take a step back Barbara.

I'm going to take a picture.

I look at you and I think of a Leonardo painting.

BARBARA: I don't know how to take that!

AYMERIC: May I?

BARBARA: What are you doing?

AYMERIC: Just your face.

He rearranges her hair.

It's as if we already knew each other.

She moves away, strumming some notes.

BARBARA sings the beginning of a song by JULIETTETE DEMBA. –

'When the sky gets dark
And the lights go out
In so many cities
In so many countries
Any hope of revolution
Is lost forever.'

The flash of the photo.

4.

*Morning, on the Balbek stage. LUCA and NICOLE, text in hand. EVA
and BARBARA are in the stalls. FABIEN MÜLLER at the entrance.*

NICOLE: 'Has humanity learned from the sacrifices and
sufferings, from a people's despair, have they understood
the meaning, the warning, the duties imposed by these
times?

Republicans turning the Republic over to its enemies

Bureaucrats stifling courage and freedom, audacity and
faith

Pragmatic politicians, deaf to the magic of the word, blind
to the power of the idea, struck dumb before the force of
the mind

Economic fetishists for whom the moral force of the people and the great impulses of

humanity, the thirst for freedom, justice and beauty, are nothing but vices to be shunned

No, they learned nothing – all forgotten and no lessons learned

Barbarity triumphs, nationalism, racial hatred dims eyes, feelings and hearts

Always the same absurd belief in the coming of a strongman, a leader, a Caesar, a messiah who will perform miracles, take responsibility for the times to come, solve everyone's life, banish fear, eradicate poverty

Always the same absurd desire to find a scapegoat to take responsibility for the state of the times and bear the guilt of our own faults and our own crimes

The spiritual and moral values acquired over the centuries, at the cost of terrible suffering and struggle are turned to mockery and hatred.

Freedom, humanity, fraternity and justice are all poisonous and filthy words – let them be thrown in the garbage!

Learn the virtues of the barbarian

Crush the weak

Unlearn how to feel the suffering of others

Never forget that you were born to be an avenger

Revenge yourself for the wrongs of today, those of yesterday and those that may be done to you tomorrow!

Where is the youth of Europe?

Don't they know that the laws of the old world are in pieces? After all, they've lived through the whole slow miserable collapse.

Alive without knowing why.

Desperate for a guiding light.

For dreams worth dreaming.

And they are comforted only by the intoxication of the void.'

LUCA: There you go.

That's the opening of the show, right?

What do you think, Eva?

EVA: I think I prefer Chekhov.

FABIEN: Good text that. Excellent. It could be one of my speeches.

LUCA: You are?

FABIEN: Fabien Müller, duly elected Front Line MP and fierce defender of the city of Balbek.

EVA: And you just walk in here in the middle of rehearsal?

FABIEN: I was just checking out the room. I won't stay long, sorry. Do you rent it out?

EVA: We do not rent Mr Müller.

FABIEN: And it wouldn't be possible to do that in the future?

EVA: This is not a village hall.

FABIEN: It's a publicly funded space.

EVA: Dedicated to the art of theatre.

FABIEN: Sorry I disturbed you. Allow me to say hello properly. Madam. Sir.

NICOLE shakes his hand.

LUCA and BARBARA don't.

EVA: Such an elegant exterior.

FABIEN: And very elegant backstage, incredible, isn't it?

EVA: But so ugly on the inside.

FABIEN: Now I think you're getting confused with your own fantasies. So who wrote that text?

LUCA: It's by Ernst Toller.

EVA: A German writer. He was an antifascist revolutionary communist.

FABIEN: So, if I understand correctly, it wouldn't be possible to hire this room for a meeting?

EVA: No.

FABIEN: Then all that remains is for me to apologise for disturbing you.

AYMERIC enters with a plastic bag.

AYMERIC: I found this in front of the theatre.

He puts the bag on the ground.

EVA: What is it?

AYMERIC: Take a look.

EVA: Can't you just tell me?

AYMERIC: Don't you want to look?

LUCA: A head.

AYMERIC: Exactly.

NICOLE: Oh my God!

LUCA: A pig's head if that makes you feel any better.

EVA: Who put a pig's head in front of my theatre?

AYMERIC: I have a theory about that.

LUCA: You have a theory?

AYMERIC: It's an inside job.

EVA: What?

AYMERIC: Someone on the inside.

EVA: Why would Michael do such a thing?

BARBARA: Nothing to say, Mr. Müller?

FABIEN: What do you want me to say? You should go to the police.

BARBARA: You are an elected official.

FABIEN: I don't know why you're having a go at me.

BARBARA: This just feels like the kind of stunt your party members are so fond of.

FABIEN: Excuse me, I don't think we've been introduced.

BARBARA: Barbara Bauer.

FABIEN: Are you Anna Bauer's daughter?

BARBARA: I am.

FABIEN: I'm going to be on the radio with her. We're doing a thing on culture and populism. How funny.

BARBARA: Should I repeat my question?

FABIEN: I don't see any political point to doing this. Neither I nor my party has anything to do with this sort of imbecile behaviour. It looks like mental illness to me. The police station is a two-minute walk away.

EVA: I don't suppose there's a message with the head? Something classy as favoured by your youth wing, Mr Müller like, 'We'll string you all up by the balls'?

FABIEN: I'm leaving. I might drop in at the police station myself. To file a complaint about slander.

FABIEN MÜLLER exits.

Silence.

MICHAEL: Hello.

He goes to cross.

He stops

What?

EVA: Where have you been?

MICHAEL: I just did my workshop at the care home.

AYMERIC: Someone dumped a pig's head in front of the theatre.

MICHAEL: So what?

AYMERIC: So you don't have any idea who might have done that?

MICHAEL: No.

AYMERIC: Your friend came by. Fabien Müller.

MICHAEL: I'm not interested.

He goes off to the dressing rooms.

LUCA: We have to do something.

EVA: I'm going to go and report it.

She exits.

Silence.

NICOLE: *(Looking at the pig's head.)* So disgusting.

AYMERIC: And yet so delicious.

(To the pig's head.) – Who's this?
Angels and ministers of grace defend us!
Be thou a spirit of health or goblin damned,
Bring with thee airs from heaven or blasts from hell,
Be thy intents wicked or charitable,
Thou comest in such a questionable shape
That I will speak to thee.
O, answer me!
Let me not burst in ignorance, but tell
Why thy canonised bones, hearsed in death,
Have burst their cerements;
What may this mean,
That thou, dead corse, again in complete steel
Revisits thus the glimpses of the moon,
Making night hideous and we fools of nature,
So horridly to shake our disposition
With thoughts beyond the reaches of our souls?
Say why is this? Wherefore? What should we do?

BARBARA: What's that?

AYMERIC: *Hamlet.*

BARBARA: I don't like it.

AYMERIC: Shakespeare?

23

BARBARA: People putting pigs' heads outside theatres.

AYMERIC picks up a copy of the text.

NICOLE: 'Barbarity triumphs, nationalism, racial hatred dims eyes, feelings and hearts

Where is the youth of Europe?

Don't they know that the laws of the old world are in pieces? After all, they've lived through the whole slow miserable collapse.

Alive without knowing why.'

NICOLE: What do you think, Barbara?

BARBARA: It's really beautiful.

NICOLE: You don't seem convinced.

BARBARA: It's politics. Always makes me uncomfortable. It's always just who shouts loudest, isn't it?

AYMERIC: It'll be a huge hit, Barbara. A triumph.
A three-hour running time and a blaze of glory finale. Ah, you don't know how it feels at curtain, Barbara. What a feeling. Lights down. Nerves in the wings. And the applause begins. Bam. Bam. Bam. Like a gigantic heart starting to beat. Bam. Bam. Bam. First bow. Second bow. Third bow. Fourth bow.

NICOLE: BRAVO! BRAVO! BRAVO!

LUCA: WHERE IS THE YOUTH OF EUROPE?

AYMERIC: That moment backstage, when you know the applause hasn't died down and it isn't going to die down and it gets louder and louder as you exit after the third bow and return for the ritual triumph of the fourth.

NICOLE AND LUCA: BRAVO! BRAVO! BRAVO!

AYMERIC: And now this really is a very special moment
     Barbara after that fourth call, when you go backstage, and
     you hear this sort of modulation in the crowd and a kind
     of frenzied animalistic howling starts. BRAVO. BRAVO.
     BRAVO.

NICOLE: BRAVO! BRAVO! BRAVO!

AYMERIC: The screams when you come back for the fifth
     call, people standing, trance-like, hysterical, BRAVO,
     BRAVO, BRAVO, there you are in the light, at the
     centre of the world, in the only place in the world really
     worth being, BRAVO, BRAVO! That moment at the
     fifth call when you know that you've won and there are
     a few jealous people dotted about, a pack of miserable
     scabby dogs, dotted about here and there, and there, and
     they're starting to think this is going on a bit but they
     can't deny the sheer scale of the TRIUMPH and, jealous
     as they are, they're still forced to join in the applause
     because THE THING ABOUT APPLAUSE, and you
     must never forget this Barbara, because applause is a
     MASS PHENOMENON. IT'S CROWD HYSTERIA
     IT'S A MASS PHENOMENON YES! YES! CROWD
     HYSTERIA! BRAVO! BRAVO! THE MASS! And the
     people who are jealous are too scared to leave so they
     stick with the crowd and pat their hands together like
     feeble old idiots. And you start to think a sixth call would
     bring on a merciful death for them.

NICOLE: Six! Six! Six!

AYMERIC: And this time you can come back slowly, no
     need to run, show them you've given everything, tired
     but happy. Hair a bit ruffled, satisfied, exhausted perhaps
     but grateful, like after a really good fuck, and so they
     understand the effort you've been making. And at this
     point you can allow yourself a rather naff gesture, Barbara,

and this is absolutely forbidden before a sixth call. Anyone who does it at the second bow is a total loser and doing it at the third is just pathetic. I'm talking of course about that thing where you clap along with the audience or, naffer still, actually applaud *them*! And at the seventh bow, the audience admits total defeat. They've lost the battle. They lay down their arms and you may allow yourself to give them a little clap. Well done, audience, well done for clapping so long but can we maybe go home to bed now?

NICOLE: JUST ONE MORE!

AYMERIC: You can smile a bit less on this last one, like a dad looking at his kids and going it really is bedtime now and you've had at least three stories already so thank you and good night. The applause dies away and you go back to the dressing rooms. Everyone's high-fiving like a great big football team and at that point you can mark it on the wall or in your little black book: 'Eight curtain calls plus standing ovation.' And that's when you know, for sure and certain, that you're going to be a star.

5.

LUCA and MICHAEL in the lobby of the theatre.

MICHAEL looks out at the night.

LUCA: What are you looking at, Michael?

MICHAEL: Spring's coming, the real people.

LUCA: What real people?

MICHAEL: The crowd. Out on the streets, growing, getting bigger and bigger. An infinite crowd full of joy. With flags. The people. At last. The real people of this country.

LUCA: It's raining Michael. There's no one left out on the streets. Balbek's a small town and no one cares. People go home very early. They're unhappy and they vote wrong. You're on the wrong track.

MICHAEL: You're the ones dying out.

LUCA: We're doing our work.

MICHAEL: On the rise of 'fascism'? Going to teach the whole world a lesson. Again.

LUCA: We want to talk about the elections.

MICHAEL: With him?

LUCA: With Aymeric.

MICHAEL: This guy has no idea about anything. He'd sell his mum and dad if he had to.

LUCA: We're not enemies, Michael.

MICHAEL: I'm not sure about that.

He exits

PART TWO

LOVE AND POLITICS

1.

JULIETTETE: The second time I met Aymeric was at Anna
Bauer's house by the sea

He'd come with Barbara

They'd just met.

There we were

Early evening

At the home of the Artistic Director of a large theatre in
the capital

Anna was taking a work call.

Aymeric took a look around

As if he was used to all this.

As if he wasn't impressed.

As if he belonged and this was his natural habitat

And in the longing that I saw on his face to insinuate
himself into this world

No matter what it took,

I felt a connection with him.

2.

Evening, seaside, ANNA BAUER's villa.

AYMERIC: Carpet. Tables. Sculptures. Carriage clocks. Velvet covers. Great golden mirrors. Shrubbery. Sculpted pathways. Luxury. Elegance

BARBARA: Yes, that's it. Welcome to Mummy's place. Welcome, Aymeric.

AYMERIC: There was nothing at my father's house. He always owed money. All he did was moan about the world. He'd open a bottle and then another and then another and then another. And my sister and I drank some of it surreptitiously so that he wouldn't drink too much, and I'd be half drunk and thinking, 'I've got to get out of this, I have to get away.'

BARBARA: Come on, Aymeric, I'll introduce you to my mother.

3.

Living room of the villa.

JULIETTEte, THÉO MARBER, NICOLE, AYMERIC and BARBARA.

Enter ANNA.

ANNA: Here I am. Sorry, sorry. Work just eats up my life.

BARBARA: Aymeric, this is my mother.

AYMERIC: I've heard a lot about you.

BARBARA: Aymeric is an actor in Balbek.

NICOLE: With me in the resident company.

ANNA: So you know Juliette?

JULIETTETE: Aymeric loved my show.

AYMERIC: It was fabulous.

ANNA: And you probably know Théo.

THÉO: Théo Marber.

AYMERIC: By reputation.

THÉO: I saw you somewhere, didn't I? Have I ever seen you act?

AYMERIC: Yes, it's possible.

NICOLE: Maybe in Balbek?

THÉO: I don't think so.

ANNA: In *The Seagull*, directed by Eva.

THÉO: Oh, yes, I remember. You were excellent as Treplev. I remember. A little young but ferocious, yes. Didn't I write something? Did I write something?

AYMERIC: I don't think so.

THÉO: No, I didn't.

NICOLE: You must come and see our *Cherry Orchard*. Opens in two months.

THÉO: We'll see.

ANNA: Please, let's sit.

AYMERIC: Why is she looking at me like that?

NICOLE: Relax, Aymeric.

AYMERIC: As if she were judging me.

NICOLE: It's just that she sees the gulf between you.

AYMERIC: I'll cross it.

ANNA serves drinks.

THÉO: Cheers. To the Balbek Theatre.

ALL: TO THE BALBEK THEATRE.

They drink.

ANNA: And have you been working in Balbek long?

AYMERIC: Three years now.

ANNA: They're challenging places; it's so important to keep doing theatre there.

NICOLE: It was seeing Aymeric on stage that made me want to become an actress. Do you remember? I had no idea what I was going to do with my life. I was in high school. There was a school trip. And I saw Aymeric. What play was it again?

AYMERIC: *Ivanov.*

NICOLE: *Ivanov.* That's it. And I saw it. And I just felt that there was something going on there that was so much bigger than my little life, the school corridors and the classrooms. I was dizzy. At the end of the show people applauded and I was like, in shock. It took me several minutes to come round. And I decided that would be my life. Aymeric was invited to the school to talk about theatre so I spoke to him about it. I told him how I felt. And now we're working on *The Cherry Orchard.* He's Lopakhin and I'm Varya.

AYMERIC: But we'd like to do something else.

BARBARA: Aymeric and Nicole have an idea for a show on the rise of fascism.

NICOLE: Have you seen the film of the attack, Anna?

JULIETTETE: They were plainclothes police officers.

THÉO: Who were?

JULIETTETE: The militants who attacked the refugee camp. Some of them were plainclothes police officers. More than 30,000 people are supposed to be coming on this demo to defend the white race. There are more and more of these fascists and nobody seems to care. But it's not really their thing at the New Theatre.

ANNA: What?

JULIETTETE: A bit full on, in your face, political.

ANNA: Why do you say that, Juliette?

JULIETTETE: You're more into form and formal work, I don't know how to describe it.

ANNA: Into Art, you mean?

JULIETTETE: I can just hear that capital letter.

ANNA: Aesthetic research.

AYMERIC: The two can go together.

JULIETTETE: So they say.

ANNA: Juliettete instead of talking rubbish, couldn't you play something for us?

JULIETTETE: Any time a black woman starts talking politics, someone always asks her to sing.

ANNA: Barbara is your biggest fan.

JULIETTETE: I thought that was you.

ANNA: Audiences are so fickle, my love.

BARBARA: What the hell is wrong with you two?

JULIETTETE: We've been sulking at each other all morning but everything's going to be fine with a little gospel.

ANNA: I'm going to open another bottle.

JULIETTETE: I'll sing if Aymeric accompanies me.

AYMERIC: I've got a voice like a frog.

NICOLE: You're such a liar! He's such a liar! He's got a beautiful voice and he plays the piano perfectly.

AYMERIC: Oh, not really.

JULIETTETE: Some other time then.

She goes to put on some music. ANNA brings the drinks, helped by BARBARA and NICOLE.

ANNA: It's very casual. Just help yourselves. Drinks and canapés. Do you like oysters?

THÉO: Stand back, I want at least six.

ANNA: The white wine's here. Barbara, can you give me a hand?

They serve drinks.

THÉO: So, things are good in Balbek?

AYMERIC: Yes.

THÉO: The AD's a bit hysterical, isn't she?

AYMERIC: I wouldn't want to be disloyal.

THÉO: She's a bitch.

AYMERIC: She's demanding.

THÉO: Cheers.

They toast.

THÉO: Between you and me, what irritates me right now in theatre is that it's really only for women. And not just the theatre, by the way. They're everywhere. Women here, women there. If you're a woman, good for you, but if you're black too that's the absolute jackpot. You've missed your moment, I'm afraid. There's no way a straight white man can be a star these days. But the patriarchy has survived worse, hasn't it, Anna?

JULIETTETE: Look at these two wretched victims of contemporary society.

THÉO: Am I annoying you, Juliette?

JULIETTETE: How extremely perceptive of you, Marber, but I didn't want to interrupt your misogynistic flow.

THÉO: Now, young Aymeric, did you ever do your national service?

AYMERIC: No.

THÉO: So you don't know how to use a gun? Would you know how to handle an AK47? Could you reload a Kalashnikov? No, it's all tweets and shares and likes and social media. Come on. Champagne!

He gets up, goes to get another bottle.

BARBARA: I don't understand what you see in him.

NICOLE: What did I say?

BARBARA: Sitting there staring at him with your mouth hanging open, as if he was God.

NICOLE: He's politically incorrect, I like that.

BARBARA: He's just a jerk.

NICOLE: He's one of our greatest critics.

BARBARA: Misogynistic, self-centred, frustrated.

NICOLE: You're so straitlaced; no deviant thoughts allowed!

THÉO comes back with a bottle of champagne.

THÉO: Chekhov saw the Russian revolution coming. The end of tsarism. His bourgeois characters know that they're living in the end times. And they complain and they whine because the great movement that's coming, the great revolution, is not for them. They're too old already. They're from yesterday's world. They feel that their economic and political system is in crisis and will soon disappear, that a great upheaval is coming. They'd like to be characters in Shakespeare. With epic energy and a cosmic dimension. Cruelty. The strength to hate. But they're only Chekhov characters; sick, neurotic, trapped in time, sarcasm and self-hatred. That's why our current pathetic age worships Chekhov. We recognise our own powerlessness in him. And because we're back in the 19th century, facing fundamental questions. Endemic poverty. The rich are ridiculously rich. The poor get poorer and poorer. We'd like to do something about it, but we're all sensitive and we know we have no place in the world that's coming. So we just feel gently sorry for ourselves, we rock back and forth and cry on the shoulders of our friends, grappling with this devastating question: 'Could life have been different? Or does it have to be like this?'

JULIETTETE: I hate Chekhov. The duty of an artist today is to reflect the world we live in, how can you be an artist and not represent your times?

ANNA: I love him.

AYMERIC: You love him.

JULIETTETE: Of course you do.

ANNA: It was *The Three Sisters* that first made me love theatre.

AYMERIC: What do you make of Ernst Toller?

ANNA: There are some nice passages but it's a little dated, don't you think?

BARBARA: Aymeric, can I show you something?

AYMERIC and BARBARA exit.

4.

Night, by the sea, AYMERIC and BARBARA.

AYMERIC: So this is where you spent your childhood.

BARBARA: All my school holidays.

AYMERIC: All your school holidays with that vastness in front of you.

BARBARA: Yes, the whole vast sea, in front of us. Nicole and I used to pretend we were sailing off around the world for twenty years.

AYMERIC: How did you two meet?

BARBARA: Nicole always came with her parents to the same beach, we played together as kids.

AYMERIC: And today what would you dream of for twenty
    years from now?

BARBARA: To still have something to believe in. You?

AYMERIC: To still be acting.

BARBARA: What, for example?

AYMERIC: Romeo?

BARBARA: You should swap me for Juliettete then!

AYMERIC: Romeo and Barbara sounds better, doesn't it?

BARBARA: Maybe.

AYMERIC: Barbara, the moment I saw you I had the feeling
    that I knew you. I felt something between us.

BARBARA: This is going a bit fast, isn't it?

AYMERIC: I'm in character.

BARBARA: Ah.

AYMERIC: Romeo is like that. Love. Life at a thousand miles
    an hour. Speed. It's Shakespeare.

    They kiss.

5.

NICOLE: We spent the weekend at Anna's house.

    And on Monday we went to the refugee camp

    I don't know exactly what we were looking for.

    We had to be there.

To see

To take part in the event

Bear witness

Express our disapproval

Our disgust

There we were

Ruined tents as far as the eye could see

People hanging around

Volunteers trying to serve up food

Or to help in these difficult conditions

Despite the hostile presence of the police

And some demonstrators we hooked up with

'Refugees are welcome here'

Barbara and I took some pictures

We wandered round the camp

Juliettete gave some interviews

Anna too

We just wanted to say it

Say that we didn't know how to stop it

But that it couldn't be done in our name

This violence

This injustice

And Juliette and Aymeric

Anna, Barbara and I

We unfolded this banner

In front of the TV cameras

'NOT IN OUR NAME'

It started raining

And we went back to Balbek.

6.

In the bar of the Balbek theatre, a few days later.

EVA, AYMERIC and LUCA.

LUCA: *(Reads a note.)* 'What does it mean to have a
nationality? What is it like to have a different nationality?
What is it like to live in Balbek and be Ivorian? Algerian?
Syrian? Italian? Living in Balbek and being Turkish?
Polish? German? What is it like to have a nationality
different from that of the country you live in? What is a
native country? What is exile? What is a nation? What
does it mean to belong to a nation? How does it work on
a daily basis? Based on meetings and exchanges with the
inhabitants of Balbek, a group of artists from the Balbek
theatre will urgently question our ideas of nationhood
and the relationship we have with them, at a time when
tensions are running through our societies; identity
politics, nationalism, multiculturalism and social diversity.
This research will feed into a performance by theatre
artists and volunteers from the local community.'

What do you reckon?

EVA: I'm not sure you'd find all those different nationalities in Balbek.

LUCA: They're just examples.

EVA: It's a big city project, not for the countryside.

AYMERIC: You don't want to do Ernst Toller anymore?

EVA: We're not going to do Ernst Toller. We're going to do Anton Chekhov. You're free to leave, Luca if it's not for you.

LUCA: Getting out and talking to people. Trying to see more clearly what divides us. Bringing different communities to the theatre. Asking questions about what it means to live here in this country.

EVA: We shall be asking all the questions you want, Luca, and we shall do so by putting on *The Cherry Orchard.*

LUCA: What do you think, Aymeric?

AYMERIC: I'm torn.

LUCA: Torn?

AYMERIC: Luca, no one knows us.

Let's get ourselves known first.

Anna Bauer loves Chekhov.

She could support us.

LUCA: The time to talk is now. We have to reach out to people right now.

NICOLE comes in.

With a plastic bag.

NICOLE: I found this in front of the theatre.

EVA: What is it?

NICOLE: A pig's head.

EVA: It's happening again.

LUCA: It's a declaration of war.

AYMERIC: It's Michael.

NICOLE: Why Michael? He works here.

EVA: Michael is a young man who's lost his way, that's all.

AYMERIC: There are thousands of people in Balbek and millions in this country who think exactly like him.

EVA: I'm going back to the police station.

She exits.

7.

LUCA: So she went to the police station

The police shrugged their shoulders

A pig's head in front of a theatre

They didn't take her seriously.

It was the day before the national day of rage

In defence of the white race

It was a Saturday

Never thought I'd live in times like that

And we asked ourselves in the theatre

What we could do

In this small town on the fringes

Away from the cities

With no media profile

What we could do

That might reach the greatest number of people

A speech

A performance

Posters

An occupation

A die in

Nothing

That was Eva's suggestion

Nothing

'Why should we speak out at all?

Why must we do something?

Why should we rise to the enemy's bait?

Why don't you just pretend nothing's happening?'

Hordes of people

Took to the streets

Crying out in protest against their disappearance

Aymeric was ill

Feeling ill

I couldn't understand why he'd changed his mind so abruptly

Barbara and Nicole and I made a banner eventually

Which we wanted to hang out on the front of the theatre

'WE AS THEATRE ARTISTS DEPLORE THE RISE OF ALL EXTREMISMS, IN THE FACE OF THE GOVERNMENT'S HEAVY-HANDED AND REPRESSIVE POLICIES, WE EXPRESS OUR COMPLETE DISAGREEMENT WITH THE COUNCIL'S AUTHORISATION OF THIS DEMONSTRATION. CARTE BLANCHE GIVEN TO FASCISM. WE OPPOSE THE POLICIES THAT CONTRIBUTE TO THIS RETURN TO DARKNESS AND WHICH SEEK ALWAYS TO TURN THE POOREST PEOPLE AGAINST ONE OTHER. WE CALL ON AS MANY PEOPLE AS POSSIBLE TO STAND UP TOGETHER FOR THE MANY NOT THE FEW'

But Eva said no.

'We are a public institution

Yes, I know

I have to be the bad guy here

But we cannot take sides politically

Against the elected government

We believe in democracy'

8.

Evening, on the stage of the Balbek Theatre. A gun on the table, a camera.

MICHAEL films himself rehearsing.

MICHAEL: 'We are the generation who risk death because we catch someone's eye or refuse to give someone a cigarette or just look slightly wrong. We are the generation of ethnic fracture, of the total collapse of the multicultural experiment, of enforced race-mixing. We are the generation that gets hammered twice: condemned to bail out a benefits system so generous with others that it no longer works for our own people. We are the helpless victims of the baby boomers. They claimed to want to free us from the weight of tradition, knowledge and authority in school; but all they freed was themselves from their responsibilities. We don't need your history books because we have our memory. We no longer believe that Mohammed is our brother, the planet our village and humanity our family. We've discovered that we have roots, we have ancestors, and therefore a future. Our only heritage is our blood, our soil, our identity. We have come into our destiny. We're turning off the TV and taking to the streets.'

BARBARA: What are you doing, Michael?

MICHAEL: Rehearsing.

BARBARA: Shakespeare?

MICHAEL: No.

BARBARA: Aeschylus?

MICHAEL: A declaration of war.

BARBARA: Against whom?

MICHAEL: The way things are.

BARBARA: Can I stay?

MICHAEL: What about your boyfriend?

BARBARA: What?

MICHAEL: Where's your boyfriend?

BARBARA: Why are you asking me that?

MICHAEL: Are you embarrassed?

BARBARA: Why should I be? He's not well.

MICHAEL: It's all bullshit.

BARBARA: What is?

MICHAEL: His idea for doing a political play. He's completely
full of shit as always. You'll see. He'll just carry on doing
nice little well-behaved classics with no fuss.

BARBARA: I don't want to disturb you, bye.

MICHAEL: Stay, if you want. I'm just telling you, it's bullshit.
Your boyfriend's full of shit. The rise of fascism. Always
the excuse so that nothing ever really changes.

BARBARA: Why are you an actor?

MICHAEL: I don't understand.

BARBARA: Why are you in theatre?

MICHAEL: I can't believe you're asking me that question.

BARBARA: I don't see why.

MICHAEL: Why does being an actor have to mean being an
apolitical, cosmopolitan, leftie wimp?

BARBARA: Why do theatre today? That's what I'm asking you.

MICHAEL: Because the theatre is about my country. Because the real people are hurting and they're waiting for us to say it. Because I want to show my people their own story. While Aymeric's hanging out in restaurants chasing donations and partying with the latest coked up C-listers, I'm out there, I'm meeting people, I'm touring neglected places, the suburbs, the countryside, and that's where I find my people. Humiliated. Hurt. Put on a show about the rise of fascism. Help, the 1930s are back! Did you know that Hitler came to power democratically? *(He grabs the gun on the table.)* BAM BAM BAM! Who's subsidizing this shit? THE STATE. So, in poncy theatres where there's never the slightest risk of meeting any actual real people, the metropolitan elite get all excited and put on a play about the rise of fascism, a version of a classic, warning against war and fascism or an adaptation of a novel about the dangers of war and fascism. And then the elections come. Nothing changes. They feel better. They're not threatened. And off we go again. We put another coin in the slot. Meanwhile, the real people are screaming but nobody's listening. It's just pigs squealing. The 'Left Behind'? Just losers moaning on about the evils of big business and globalisation. They talk about democracy but they can't stand to be contradicted. I hate them so fucking much it makes me actually faint sometimes. I hate hypocrisy so much it nearly kills me. I can't sleep. I hate you so much. I hate you with staggering focus, if you only knew how much. A universe. A huge blaze. Redemptive. We will sweep them away. The abject left-wing middle classes. The abject right-wing middle classes. We will sweep it all away. We are the real people of this country and we can do it. We've never been listened to. White people. The white working class. The honest workers of the country. Men who love women. Women who are not ashamed to be women. Who are not ashamed to have children. Who are not ashamed to be at home. To watch their children grow up. To teach them respect for tradition. The men and women of right here who've been despised and ignored and who always vote the wrong way. We the real people. Do you understand Barbara? We will be able to speak freely, freely at last, and we won't be scared any more. We won't be ashamed. We will be in our own home. This is our home. OUR HOME. And we can take back our country for the real people.

BARBARA: Michael, you're scaring me.

MICHAEL: It's exhilarating.

BARBARA: Put the gun down, please.

MICHAEL: It's not real Barbara, it's theatre.

BARBARA: It still scares me.

MICHAEL: Can I see your skin?

BARBARA: Put it down right now.

MICHAEL: Your white skin.

BARBARA: Please.

MICHAEL: Just your shoulder, your white skin, the real people, just the top.

He uncovers her shoulder.

MICHAEL: Why don't you come with us, Barbara? You're white and if we don't do something soon we'll be replaced and our children will be speaking a foreign language.

BARBARA: I'll buy you a drink at the bar.

MICHAEL: What do you want?

BARBARA: To buy you a drink at the bar.

MICHAEL: Do you fancy me?

BARBARA: No.

MICHAEL: Why do you want to buy me a drink at the bar then?

BARBARA: To talk.

MICHAEL: You don't fancy me?

BARBARA: Calm down.

MICHAEL: Not even a little bit?

BARBARA: You intrigue me. You look exhausted.

MICHAEL: Don't patronise me.

BARBARA: Put the gun down, please. We're having a dialogue.

MICHAEL: History isn't made by dialogue.

BARBARA: If one day this country really becomes what you want it to become, I'd rather not have anything to do with it.

MICHAEL: White skin is on the verge of extinction.

BARBARA: You're delirious.

MICHAEL: We pretend it's not precious skin. The most precious thing in the world. Ivory.

He touches BARBARA's shoulder, still with the gun pointed at her.

MICHAEL: When I look at your white skin, Barbara, I see small working-class neighbourhoods. Allotments. Long walks in the fields. The work of our ancestors. When I look at your white skin. People spilling out of mass on

Sundays. The proud bodies of our fathers and mothers, proud of their work and their community. When I look at your white skin Barbara, I see the long family table for Sunday lunch. Your white skin, and clear, blue, innocent eyes. Long evenings in the countryside, the grape harvest and September skies over the vines, laughter and firm handshakes between men, the brotherhood of the real people.

AYMERIC enters.

AYMERIC: What are you doing, Barbara?

BARBARA: I'm talking to Michael.

MICHAEL: I thought you were ill, Che Guevara?

AYMERIC: I'm feeling great.

MICHAEL: So how's the show on the rise of fascism going?

AYMERIC: Want to be in it?

MICHAEL: I try to avoid certain flops.

AYMERIC: There's a great part for you, though. It's a small-town Nazi. The kind of kid who always got beaten up in the playground and still gets regular slaps.

MICHAEL: I guess the money's rolling in for this right-on crap, right?

AYMERIC: Enough to let me cast Fabien Müller.

BARBARA: That's enough, Aymeric.

AYMERIC: We could improvise a little pastoral love scene. We'll have you both be naked in a clearing, lying on Nazi flags and shouting HEIL HITLER when you come.

BARBARA: Aymeric!

AYMERIC: The fat local brownshirt and his little cutie.

MICHAEL: I'll give you ten seconds to take back what you just said.

BARBARA: We were just talking.

MICHAEL: Nine...

AYMERIC: You don't talk to the far right.

MICHAEL: Eight...

AYMERIC: You don't try to find common ground.

MICHAEL: Seven...

AYMERIC: You don't debate.

MICHAEL: Six...

AYMERIC: He's a deadly enemy.

MICHAEL: Five...

AYMERIC: And what you do to the enemy is destroy, exterminate and annihilate.

MICHAEL: Four...

AYMERIC: That's what you have to understand, Barbara.

MICHAEL: Three...

AYMERIC: What democrats will have to understand.

MICHAEL: Two...

AYMERIC: If we want to remain friends–

MICHAEL: One...

AYMERIC: – of freedom.

MICHAEL: You wanker.

AYMERIC: You piece of shit.

MICHAEL: I'm going to exterminate you. I'm going to watch you die.

BARBARA: STOP! STOP!

They fight.

BARBARA: STOP! STOP!

She exits. They continue to fight. MICHAEL has the upper hand.

MICHAEL: YOU FUCKING MIDDLE CLASS WANKER/ YOU ARTY CUNT/TRAITOR/TRAITOR/TRAITOR.

LUCA and EVA enter, followed by BARBARA.

EVA: STOP! STOP! STOP! STOP! NOT IN MY THEATRE!

LUCA rushes to separate AYMERIC and MICHAEL.

LUCA: STOP! Stop it! Calm down! Get off him, Michael! Let go of him right now.

MICHAEL: Fucking lefty motherfucker! You piece of shit!

LUCA: LEAVE IT!

AYMERIC: WE MUST WIPE OUT THIS FASCIST WE MUST DESTROY HIM.

LUCA: CALM DOWN!

AYMERIC: THE POLICE.

CALL THE POLICE.

STICK HIM IN THE CELLS.

MICHAEL: YOU SHITHEAD!

EVA: THAT'S ENOUGH. SILENCE. I REFUSE TO HAVE CONFLICT IN MY THEATRE!

MICHAEL: You say you have to fight but you can't. You just scream for the police. The same police you despise the rest of the time, always slagging them off, no respect for them at all, but you beg them for help the moment someone comes and rapes your wife.

EVA: I'M ASKING YOU TO BE QUIET, MICHAEL.

MICHAEL: It's all over. You're traitors. I hate you. I hate you. We will wipe you all out.

He runs off. A pause.

AYMERIC: I want this guy gone.

EVA: Calm down, Aymeric.

AYMERIC: It's either him or me.

LUCA: What happened?

AYMERIC: He had his hands on Barbara.

BARBARA: We were talking.

AYMERIC: YOU DON'T TALK TO THE FAR RIGHT.

EVA: What was the fight about?

AYMERIC: I can see how you are Barbara. How you all are. You've forgotten what fascism is all about. Systemic destruction. The death spiral. The thrill of destroying everything fragile, elegant, fine and tender. And you just stand there, watching. It's interesting how this man talks. From an anthropological point of view, of course, it's possible to find fascist dictatorship interesting. But deep down, you have to say no, this isn't happening again, it won't happen again. They're idiots. The left behind. You have no imagination.

EVA: What happened here, Aymeric?

BARBARA: Michael was recording a far right-wing manifesto and I was trying to understand what he believes in. Then Aymeric arrived.

AYMERIC: I'm leaving this theatre tomorrow if this guy isn't fired immediately for serious misconduct.

EVA: We can't do things like that.

AYMERIC: There is no other option.

LUCA: I don't think that's a good idea.

EVA: I'll summon him to my office tomorrow.

AYMERIC: He has to leave.

EVA: I can't fire him like that.

AYMERIC: What the hell is the matter with you? Did you hear what he said?

LUCA: You want to throw oil on the fire? Feed his paranoia?

AYMERIC: I don't know who you are anymore.

LUCA: Junior actor at publicly funded Balbek theatre fired because he dares to criticise the great left-wing actor.

AYMERIC: He insults us. He's threatening us with death.

EVA: I'll talk to him tomorrow. I can't fire someone like that. We took him in here. He's come a long way. With the demonstration and all the excitement, he's not himself.

AYMERIC: If you always calculate, instead of doing what's right, you will lose. He's not a kid, he's your enemy. It's either him or me.

EVA: Aymeric, please, there's no comparison.

AYMERIC: Either he leaves or I leave. Have a good evening.

AYMERIC exits.

PART 3

LAST DAYS IN BALBEK

1.

BARBARA: A few days

A week passed

Aymeric stayed in Balbek

And I stayed in Balbek

I don't know what I was looking for

Something was keeping me there

As if the heart of the country was beating right there

Easier to hear

Not muffled by the roar of the big city

Balbek

The streets

The old church

The clock-tower

Fields that extend as far as the eye can see

And you look at the little grey houses

And you wonder

But how can anyone stand to live here?

And then a few days go by

A week

And you find out about these lives

Amazing stories

A whole world you never suspected was there

Quite absent from our national history

I stayed in Balbek

I moved in with Aymeric

I sat in on the Chekhov rehearsals

There was something in his way of doing theatre

He seemed less sure of himself

Less arrogant than at my mother's

A theatre like a cherry orchard

That's what Eva wanted to create

It was to be her last production.

She didn't know it yet

There was something touching though a little masochistic

About the Balbek Theatre people

Giving something you don't have to someone who doesn't want it

But who gradually gets a taste for it

A theatre in Balbek

2.

AYMERIC comes out of a butcher's shop with a plastic bag. FABIEN MÜLLER is in the street.

FABIEN: And here comes the great actor

AYMERIC: Excuse me?

FABIEN: Fabien Müller, Member of Parliament for the Front Line.

AYMERIC: I didn't recognise you.

FABIEN: How is the Balbek Theatre doing?

AYMERIC: Come and see our *Cherry Orchard.*

FABIEN: Your cherry what?

AYMERIC: Chekhov's *Cherry Orchard?*

FABIEN: I was just kidding you, yes, I know Chekhov, I've heard very good things.

AYMERIC: This is our fourth and final performance tonight.

FABIEN: Can you give us a free ticket?

AYMERIC: Of course.

FABIEN: Excellent.

AYMERIC exits with the plastic bag. We hear applause in the distance.

3.

Morning, the bar of the Balbek Theatre. BARBARA with AYMERIC on his smartphone.

Applause in the distance growing louder.

AYMERIC: Nothing yet, nothing about our *Cherry Orchard,* there's a review for what's-his-name, a review for that jerk and his shitty digital show 'I want to show how new technologies have impacted our lives.' Twat. It's a rave, he won't get his ego through the door. We'll have to steer well clear of the little bastard. Every time he does something, he reckons it 'changes everything'. I can just see him rushing to post the review on his wall and waiting feverishly for the likes to arrive. I swear to you. If he died, frankly, I'd break out the champagne.

BARBARA: What the hell is wrong with you, Aymeric?

AYMERIC: The total injustice.

BARBARA: How can you talk like that?

AYMERIC: I'm not staying in Balbek.

BARBARA: I like it here.

AYMERIC: Of course you do.

BARBARA: Why, of course?

AYMERIC: You're a hipster tourist in the countryside. 'It's so cute.' 'How authentic people are.' And then you go home to Mummy.

BARBARA: You should get help.

AYMERIC: Why didn't Théo Marber come?

BARBARA: He's pathetic.

AYMERIC: I don't give a shit. Someone has to write about me. I need someone to validate me. Why don't you ask your mother to make him come?

BARBARA: They'll be here tonight.

AYMERIC: You've been saying that for a week.

BARBARA: She told me she'd be here for the last night.

AYMERIC: Barbara, tell me the truth, am I a good actor?

BARBARA: You're a good actor. You're a very good actor, Aymeric. What are you worried about? You're one of the best actors in the world. You're the best. You're perfect in the *Cherry Orchard.*

AYMERIC: I'm sorry. I'm a child. I'm being ridiculous. It's nerves.

BARBARA: Everything will be fine. My mother will come with Marber and you'll get a great review. It'll all happen one step at a time. Don't stress. You need to give yourself a break.

AYMERIC: You're ashamed of me.

BARBARA: What are you talking about? I'm Barbara and you're Romeo. Remember Aymeric?

AYMERIC: Romeo and Barbara.

She kisses him.

Applause in the distance, getting louder.

4.

The stage of the Balbek Theatre. Last night of The Cherry Orchard. Curtain call. Applause.

AYMERIC: First bow.

The cast bow and go backstage.

AYMERIC: Second bow.

The cast bow and go backstage

AYMERIC: Third bow.

The cast bow and go backstage. The applause stops.

AYMERIC: What the hell?

AYMERIC suddenly springs up alone on stage

AYMERIC: Oh! Oh! Oh! Three bows and that's it? You don't care, do you? You're not interested at all in Chekhov! You clap your hands three pathetic times and you're happy and you're off out for dinner and that's it! Do you have any idea of the work that's gone into this? What is this town? What's wrong with you? We're putting on incredible shows in this shithole!

EVA: *(From the wings.)* Aymeric! Aymeric!

AYMERIC: We're bringing you actual great ART, you fucking peasants!

EVA: Stop it, Aymeric.

AYMERIC: Great writers, great plays and all with a big reassuring smile so as not to frighten you too much and all you can manage is three pathetic little curtain calls? And your arses firmly stuck to your seats!

EVA: Aymeric STOP.

AYMERIC: Two or three semi-retired businessmen, minor civil servants, failed artists, herds of schoolchildren getting bored shitless, a few creepy old teachers.

EVA: LUCA, HELP ME.

EVA and LUCA come on to the stage and try to control him.

AYMERIC: THE MIDDLE CLASSES, YOU'RE SO BORING! YOU'RE SO BORING YOU SHOULD ALL DIE YOU'RE SO INCAPABLE OF THINKING BIG YOU BLOCK THE SLIGHTEST POSSIBILITY OF GREATNESS

LUCA: AYMERIC

AYMERIC: THE SLIGHTEST POSSIBILITY OF CHANGE

EVA: STOP THIS

AYMERIC: BUT I'M NOT A COUNTRY PRIEST, I DO ART, I DON'T DO CHARITY.

LUCA: It's okay, Aymeric, it's okay!

AYMERIC: I'm done with Balbek. I'm leaving. I'm leaving. I'm going to the city. History is happening without me. History is happening without you, peasants!

LUCA: AYMERIC STOP.

EVA: SO SORRY, LADIES AND GENTLEMEN! HE'S NOT WELL! HE'S NOT WELL! I'M SORRY!

AYMERIC: Yes, that's right, that's it, I'm having a little nervous breakdown. It's all fine, I'm an artist I'm allowed. I'm bipolar, a little crazy is chic. I'm drowning in Balbek. I'm getting fat. I'm getting ground down. But I won't be a brave little soldier, I'll be famous for my art. I'm going to make it in the big city, make movies. Everybody wants the latest thing, see, as soon as you're not the next big thing anymore, you better move on to something else pretty sharpish or the lack of success gets corrosive. And the times we live in hate that. The times we live in hate the needy. Anything that doesn't shine, anything that doesn't go fast enough. THE TIMES WE LIVE IN HATE BALBEK.

He exits.

BLACKOUT.

5.

NICOLE: Anna Bauer didn't come to see *The Cherry Orchard*

Neither did Théo Marber

And Fabien Müller wasn't there

The audience left the theatre

As if nothing had happened.

Two days later

Aymeric moved to the city

And Barbara stayed in Balbek

She travelled back and forth

The weeks passed

She wrote about the Balbek theatre

Worked with Eva

Lived through some great times and some failures

Considered doing a PhD

Her relationship with Aymeric limped on like that for a while

I had a feeling she might have been better with Luca

Simpler

More straightforward

Less talented than Aymeric

You don't make great theatre by doing the right thing

Eva often said

But you can do bad theatre and still do the right thing

And I think, deep down, Barbara, like Luca,

Preferred doing the right thing to making great theatre.

6.

Balbek, daytime, MICHAEL and LUCA, near a small church.

LUCA: What are you doing here?

MICHAEL: Keeping a lookout.

LUCA: You could come back. Apologise. Get your job back.

MICHAEL: Apologise?

LUCA: You threatened to kill us, Michael.

MICHAEL: I said what I said.

LUCA: I'd like you to come back to us.

MICHAEL: I have to stay here. The church. I have a feeling something's going to happen.

LUCA: Why would something happen?

MICHAEL: Our churches are in danger.

LUCA: Why?

MICHAEL: My parents and grandparents were married there. It's a beautiful little church. And it's in danger.

LUCA: It's not in any danger.

MICHAEL: But I know it is.

LUCA: Well I suppose there have been local government cuts and money for maintenance might be tight. But I don't think there's anything to worry about. It is a beautiful, solid little church. It's not in any danger.

MICHAEL: But I know it is.

LUCA: Michael, I like you. I spoke with your mother yesterday. She's worried.

MICHAEL: I don't want you talking to my mother.

LUCA: Michael, we got on well for a while. The first time I saw you, you were in that theatre workshop. There were only boys in the class, and I talked to you about

MICHAEL: Molière. *The Misanthrope.*

LUCA: We read some scenes.

MICHAEL: It was interesting in a small town with 30% unemployment.

LUCA: Would you have preferred to hear about Walt Disney?

MICHAEL: You wanted to make me think like you.

LUCA: I wanted us to be able to think together.

MICHAEL: You don't know anything about what's going on, what's coming. We're being replaced.

LUCA: Michael, this is bullshit. African migrants aren't going to destroy your world. How long is this going to go on? How long are you going to keep believing that your nextdoor neighbour is your enemy? You had something different about you. You were interested in things then too, really lively and I was happy when you joined us. What's the matter with you? Why are you doing this? Why are you letting these bastards manipulate you? Come back to the theatre. Eva's fine with it.

MICHAEL: Maybe you'll get it before it's too late.

LUCA: Someone said you're walking around with a gun? Do you have a gun?

MICHAEL: I'm waiting for the elections.

He exits.

PART FOUR

ASCENSION

1.

Aymeric's there now

In the big city

It's been a few weeks

He lives in a small flat

Too small and the rent's crippling

No one knows who he is

No one knows his name

He works

Goes to the New Theatre

Goes to shows

Getting a handle on who's who

Who decides

Who decrees

Who supports

Who asserts and analyses

Who's in

Who keeps the keys

No time to waste

Go for it

Live in the future

Never the present

Never the past

The next move

He knows

That no one succeeds

Just because they want to

That no one gets the breaks

Just because they deserve them

That no one makes it

Just by being in the right place at the right time

He knows

That the work is both everything and nothing

That talent always pays and never pays

He knows

That things are complicated

He lives in the 21st century in the West

He has understood that everything is connected to everything else

And nothing is

But that desire is king and to arouse desire is all that matters

It's so nice of you to find a moment for me, JULIETTE.

It's a pleasure to meet you.

I'd so love to work with you.

I have a busy schedule.

Could we work something out?

Contact Mario for me, he's a good guy, he'll introduce you to people

He contacts Mario

He's interesting,

Says Mario

Who is?

Asks Anna Bauer

Aymeric Dupré

And Mario gives him a job

It's the story of a man who goes off to work one morning but gets off the bus before his stop for no reason and heads back the way he came

On the first night

At the New Theatre

The critic Théo Marber is there

And so is Barbara

She takes care of Marber.

She knows what she's doing

She welcomes him

She gets him a drink.

First bow

Second bow

Third bow

So what did you think?

Aymeric was excellent but I'm not sure about the play

Are you going to write a column?

Now, now, you're not supposed to ask that, Barbara my dear

Oh I think I'm allowed, Théo.

That was great, darling, you have to meet Max! Do you know Max? You don't know Max?

Tell him I told you to call him.

Marber, what can I get you?

Champagne, Anna, champagne!

And so the night goes on

A dazzling night

At the New Theatre

And Aymeric sparkling brightest of all

And by the time Théo staggers drunkenly into a taxi

Around one in the morning

He's pretty clear on everything he needs to write and think about Aymeric Dupré

'Remarkable, a highly promising actor, remember the name'

Are there any more?

That's about it.

So you're not ashamed of me now

I've never been ashamed of you

You were ashamed because I wasn't an A-list actor

That's all in your head.

And in your mother's! What are you doing?

My stuff. I'm taking the five o'clock train to Balbek.

Already?

You're coming next weekend, right?

I'm swamped.

We see each other less and less.

I'm doing what I can Barbara, things are moving. Next weekend. Promise!

And things are moving

And a year goes by

And Aymeric gets work

Meets Max

What theatre needs today is insurrection! Theatre must be larger than life

Aymeric says to him

He's so interesting

Says Max

And he casts him in a Chekhov

And Aymeric works

And on the first night of *Uncle Vanya*

Théo Marber is there again.

But this time Barbara stays in Balbek

First bow

Second bow

Third bow

Fourth bow

Aymeric, you were quite brilliant.

Thank you, Théo

Chekhov had such a sense of the coming Russian revolution and all the things that were on their way to ravage the 20th century. That's what you capture so brilliantly, Aymeric, this sense of a gaping maw sucking the character into a catastrophic future. The characters have a looming premonition of total destruction, of the great catastrophe, in a sense, they're already dead but they have no idea what to do about it except complain! And that's what we love best, these days, not having a clue what to do, isn't it? You're really great Aymeric, the play is a masterpiece and your performance is dazzling! Cheers!

And did you enjoy the show, Juliettete?

Oh yes, very much

Cheers

Cheers

To Aymeric

To Aymeric

And the night goes on

And the party starts

Anna I love you and I've never told you

What's the matter with you, Marber?

You're the only one in this whole shitshow who's held on to what's really important in art

Théo's totally pissed! Can someone get a taxi?

Where are you sleeping tonight, Nicole?

I booked a hotel

Let's get a taxi

Who wants a taxi? How many taxis?

And Marber leaves at half one in the morning

Completely smashed

He's had a wonderful evening

Are you going to write something?

Now, now, you don't ask that

And the taxis start up

And roll out across the city

And Aymeric goes home with Nicole and he wonders

As he takes her clothes off

If Marber's going to write something, will he write
something

He has to write something.

He has to make me matter

*'Kill for a ticket, theatre at its highest level, Dupré transcends the
stage'*

Any others?

A double page with a great big photo of you

Nicole, why not stay on another day?

I have workshops all week

What about Eva? How is she?

She really needs to go

How long have we been saying that?

I bumped into Fabien Müller in the week, he dropped by the theatre. And when Eva started getting angry, he said he thought it would be a good idea for you to be Artistic Director

They'll shut it down if they win the elections

That's not what he said

So what did he say?

That you were the pride of the city.

Artistic Director

I'm not staying anyway. Couldn't you get me a part somewhere?

I'll see

I have to get going. And, uh, I'd rather keep this just between us.

Sure

For Barbara's sake

I've forgotten already

People know your name

But not your face

And people know your face

But not your name

My job

It's about bringing the two together

Attaching your name to your face

Says his publicity guy Ben Ryner

It's not cheap.

But Aymeric pays

Because he knows that art is not entertainment

It's a business.

And that time is against him

And that the public is a wild animal

Always hungry

And

Always

Always

Wanting more

The public is a magnificent wild animal

That can carry you majestically to every corner of the world

One day

And then rip your head off with a casual paw the next

And Aymeric now knows that he's down there in the arena

He moves to a bigger flat

He can feel that things are changing

'People look at me differently already

They think they know me from somewhere'

And when he goes past

People slowly take their hands out of their pockets

In anticipation

Maybe he'd do a selfie?

And Aymeric wants to run with the beast

And tame it

'I'm suffocating here'

Says Aymeric

Some air

Some air

Something bigger

It's very good of you to find a moment for me

It's a pleasure to meet you

I'd just love to work with you

My schedule's pretty-

We'll work something out.

Is this the play about the rise of fascism?

I was thinking more like a Shakespeare.

Romeo?

And JULIETTE.

And what would I play?

I was thinking more like Hamlet and you'd play Ophelia.

A black Ophelia?

It'll be really urgent.

Oh fuck off

Laughs

Kisses

Embraces

Romeo is like that

Love

Life at a thousand miles an hour

Speed

It's Shakespeare.

'And there's something really sad about success'

Thinks Aymeric

A few months later

Two years after his arrival in the capital

As the party heaves

In this super cool city centre luxury flat

Celebrities, hypocrisy and tears

Money, show business and big business

'The culture of my generation' Aymeric thinks

But he banishes the thought

Because melancholy is not the order of the day

For those who want success

And he thinks of his father

Back in the suburbs of Balbek

A small-town accountant out on the fringes of the age

And he thinks of the phrase he'd repeat endlessly

To himself, as a miserable teenager shut up in his room

'I've got to get out of here

I've got to leave all this behind'

And his father appears

Stumbling about in his memories

And cursing the world

And the weight of his own failure

And Aymeric remembers the laughter

And the jokes

When his father would stagger drunkenly out of the bar

To take his son home

'Home, son'

But it was ten-year-old Aymeric, who brought his father home

'This way, Dad.'

And as the party roars

In this city centre luxury flat

After a first night triumph

Among all these radiant and stunning faces

Filled with possibilities

At the very heart of the times

Smack in the centre

Aymeric suddenly clenches his fists

And dreams of solar vengeance

Of total massacre

Of reducing it all to a waste of ashes

But it's night outside

Glorious night

And everyone looks great

And the women are beautiful

And so are the men

And everyone has stuff that they have to forget

Everyone has images of death and wars and unresolved conflicts

And you have to know how to carry this off, Aymeric

And not repeat your father's failure

Because tonight the world

Is like a luxury art gallery

Sacred

Sacred

Sacred

Sacred

Because tonight the world

Aymeric

Is exactly how you've always wanted it to be

'Aymeric Dupré is a revelation, staggering, a quite breath-taking performance, It's a masterpiece, I'm still shaking'

Any others?

That's about all of them.

Can you take your clothes off now?

I'm exhausted, Aymeric.

You read me my reviews and you take off your clothes

Keep your fantasies to yourself

It's just fun

I'm depressed.

We're lovers, aren't we?

The state of the world depresses me

Everyone listens to you, JULIETTE, everyone loves you, you're a star. The lights go down, you're centre stage, you close your eyes and sing.

Can you hear yourself?

Music protects you.

I'm talking about politics and you're talking about just ignoring it?

That's not what I'm saying, you're twisting it

Are you going?

I'm meeting up with Anna.

It's weird the relationship you have.

Who asked you?

And the days go by

One show after another

The reviews are rave.

It's like a dream

He no longer touches the ground

He parties

He is finally rid of the weight of Balbek

And the little throbbing guilt he feels about the theatre
people there

Because you can hate yourself when you're a failure

But not when you're winning

'It's still not quite perfect'

He thinks at another glittering party

'Why is there always something sad

About success?'

He thinks again

As he says what he thinks of Louis' latest show

Says what he thinks of Louise's latest show

Says what he thinks of Alfonso's latest show

Aymeric

Says what he thinks of Paola's latest show

Aymeric, I'm going home

Says what he thinks of Anna's project

Says what he thinks of the latest piece by the Collectif
Couette

Aymeric I'm going to go

Adores Jacque's latest

AYMERIC, I'M SICK OF THIS

Gives his take on what Jim thinks of Paul's short film

I'm going

Says what he thinks of a book he hasn't read

As Barbara leaves the flat around two in the morning

And the image of his father

Appears staggering around the suburbs of Balbek

Home, son. Come on, let's go, son.

I love you, son.

WHAT'S THE MATTER?

WHAT'S THE MATTER?

LEAVE ME ALONE

WHAT'S THE MATTER WITH ALL OF YOU?

LEAVE ME ALONE

I'M DOING MY JOB

I DO MY FUCKING JOB.

WHAT ARE YOU ALL LOOKING AT ME LIKE THAT?

LET ME DO MY WORK.

I'M JUST AN ACTOR.

The city outside

A comet hurtling through the starry void

'And there's something sad about it.'

Thinks Aymeric, safely in the toilet

On the throne

As the shit slips away

And the party roars on outside in the flat.

Something sad.

All those people who seemed inaccessible to him yesterday

Who seemed to live in a higher world

Unattainable and remote

Carrying entire cities within them

World travel

Cultural treasures

The whole great history of art

Well they're boring now

'They stink of mortality.'

He thinks

Quoting Shakespeare

While he wipes his arse

And he flushes

And goes back to the party

Convinced now that this isn't all there is

He must go further

Higher

He has to aim higher

There has to be something

Something more

If he's going to be

Completely

Safe

Shielded

Spared

By glory

'Insatiable, ubiquitous, tireless, enriching theatre, TV, and cinema equally with his genius'

Any others?

Yes. 'Fascist attacks on university protestors, new restrictions on the rights of asylum seekers, police repression and violence, arrests of journalists, censorship, the Front Line at 58% in the polls'

Are you trying to make me feel guilty?

You asked, I'm just telling you.

I don't see why you're talking to me like this

Do you know what I'm working on at the moment, Aymeric?

Why are you asking me that?

What else I'm doing besides reading out your reviews?

Are you jealous?

Do you know what I'm doing in Balbek?

I don't want to play that game.

What I've been doing there for the last two years?

You're working with Eva.

But you're not interested.

Barbara, please.

I'm writing a thesis on the decentralisation of theatre in the 21st century, on all this little-known work and on all the people who've been affected by the Balbek Theatre. It would be nice if you'd speak up for Balbek, you could get the press to come.

I will.

Eva's being slaughtered. People only want her to programme musicals and stand-ups off the telly but she's holding out. It would be nice if you could show some support, now that you're sort of well known.

I said I'll come.

This is the third time you've said it though, and then you cancel at the last minute.

Well pardon me for being in work.

Even if you don't come back to Balbek and the press don't come, this work will still matter. You have to learn how to love the shade Aymeric, there are things going on there. You'll regret it someday.

Amen.

You can't see anything. You can't hear anything. You don't notice anything. You have no idea what's going on in real life. All you know is the stage, dressing rooms, first night drinks, film sets. Panting like a dog for your next part.

I'm an actor Barbara, it's my job, enough with the clichés, thanks.

I really wonder if you loved me. If you ever actually loved me at all. Did you? Wasn't I just a prop? You only really loved me for my mother. What are you smiling about? Sounds like a bad play, doesn't it? You know nothing about how I spend my time, do you? I don't know what I have in common with you.

No, maybe nothing actually.

Maybe nothing.

Don't let me keep you.

2.

ANNA: My daughter's not happy

She can't sit still

Can't put her mind to anything

She's wearing herself away

Looking for a way out

An escape route

The woman I love isn't happy

We seem to get worse and worse at loving each other

Something's slowly twisting inside me

And inside the country

More and more

Even my work doesn't take me out of myself now

Stuff happens

We talk about it for a couple of days.

And then forget

I get invited to do an interview to talk about culture
and art

And the other guest is

Fabien Müller

The Front Line candidate for the Presidency.

*The country is crying out, ordinary people are living in terrible
conditions and there's this tiny, gold-plated metropolitan elite
who couldn't be further from how real people live and here they
are giving us yet another lesson in tolerance by calling us Nazis.
You are cut off from just about every aspect of people's real lives.
You talk to us about sharing, about equality between men and
women, but you support policies that destroy the lives of hardworking people. You're obsessed with migrants because they're
foreigners, but you don't give a toss about the millions of working
people struggling with poverty in your own country and you
blithely support policies that actively contribute to their misery.*

*I have no problem with reality, Mr Müller. I live in the same
world you do. We live in a system where an ever smaller minority
of people holds more wealth and power than the vast majority
of the rest of humanity. And you blame everything on people on
poverty wages, the unemployed, entirely powerless people. Why
do you set the most vulnerable in our society against each other?
Why do you make people believe that our way of life is in deadly
danger from migrants; women, men and children in terrible
distress and want? The sort of politics you practise has never
achieved anything. You promise prosperity to those who have
nothing but all you can really offer them is misery and ignorance
and the end of everything.*

But of course he's not really talking to me.

He's using me.

Speaking through me

I look at him

And it's suddenly as if I'm hearing him from a long way off

As if the world I live in

Has absolutely nothing in common with his

And we're flying faster and further apart

In the name of tolerance and multiculturalism, you support religions that absolutely oppose your principles of secularism and your so-called humanist political theories. What hypocrisy, you leave your borders undefended and then watch thousands of people die trying to cross them. Sure, you save one or two and take a selfie to make yourself feel better. This great and glorious nation must free itself, have the courage to be truly itself once more, and dazzle the world.

My daughter isn't happy

I'm in love with a woman who's younger than me

And seems further and further away every day

I feel old

I don't know how to age

I don't know how people do it

Sometimes I dream of going off somewhere to hide

Deep in some great forest

So no one can see me anymore

Do you understand?

Couldn't you be a bit gentler?

A little more sensitivity?

Something

I don't know

A little more humane

We could just sit here quietly together

But he wouldn't be quiet

Screaming at the whole world

So I went out

Into the streets

Quietly

Into the fresh air.

PART FIVE

THE DEAL

1.

The city. A café, AYMERIC and FABIEN MÜLLER.

FABIEN: My dear Aymeric, I wanted to talk to you about something. You and I have this in common, this precious plot of land, Balbek. Lost in the depths of the country. The town where I spent my childhood days. My constituency. I want to breathe new life into the Balbek Theatre. I'd like you to take over as Artistic Director.

AYMERIC: I don't know if I could make the compromises you'd need

FABIEN: Why would you say that? Who said anything about compromise?

AYMERIC: What's your vision for this theatre?

FABIEN: For you to run it.

AYMERIC: I want to do *Hamlet*.

FABIEN: That's exactly what I want too.

AYMERIC: I won't make any concessions.

FABIEN: I admire independence.

AYMERIC: I will never back down on my art.

FABIEN: No one's asking you to.

AYMERIC: Balbek is a bit isolated.

FABIEN: We have a major project to modernise the rail links. We're going to break down the centralisation of the country. That is the least we owe to our constituents.

We're going to win this election, Aymeric, we're going to be in power.

I'll let you think about it.

2.

JULIETTETE: And it was around this time

That I went to the big annual awards ceremony

I went with Anna

And the audience

I couldn't help noticing

Almost completely white

Actually, I always notice it

I live with a white woman

I'm used to it

The light streamed down over all the naked white backs

All the carefully made up faces

The famous and the fashionable

A truly fabulous ceremony

Sparkling

Rustling

The perfume heavy on the air

Fragrant actors and directors

Fragrant actresses and artists

All fragrant

Anna and I were fragrant

We had our picture taken

Sitting there all elegant and famous in the middle of the audience

And then the host started by explaining

That the winners' speeches had been getting a bit too long every year

And that they were going to be super strict on timings tonight

He explained that as soon as the allotted time was up

Someone would come and touch the errant speaker on the face

Just a little tap on the winner's face

To make them stop

And a black guy on a Segway

This kind of stand up rolling thing

Comes out on stage to demonstrate

And everyone's laughing

And the ceremony starts

And any time the winners

Best actor

Best play

Best music

Best set design

Any time they went over the two minutes

The black guy on his Segway came zooming out

And tapped them on the face to laughter and applause

A black guy with no lines

A super polite black guy

Whirring out to touch the fragrant bourgeoisie

To shut them up

Just for a laugh

Look out, here he comes again, there he is, no, don't touch me, I'm off!

The boldest would slip in a last quick word about minority representation

And head off backstage, trophy in hand, so proud of themselves

Anna didn't say anything

I felt her tensed up.

Others too

I'm not comfortable with this, Anna

We were kind of stunned

And there I was

One of the only black people in a crowd of over 1,000

Can't take a joke, is that it?

No sense of humour?

In such an elegant country

So refined

So fragrant

In this sumptuous ceremony

Amongst the famous and the fashionable and the powerful

Honouring the best shows

The best artists in the country

And the big black man's back on his Segway

Helpless laughter everywhere

Tickling any speakers who go over their time

And everybody laughed

And I was ashamed

What the hell are you doing?

Why did you agree to do this, bro?

Why are you here?

Why is either of us here?

And something cracked inside me

And when it was Aymeric's turn

To go up and accept the Best Actor award

When he went on stage

And kicked off his speech

I got up

And I went out

Into the streets

Quietly

Into the fresh air.

3.

The lobby of the Balbek theatre, election day. BARBARA and LUCA. EVA enters.

EVA: You didn't vote? In a presidential election?

LUCA: What's the point?

BARBARA: I did.

LUCA: My aunt is a racist homophobic neo-colonialist who's in favour of cutting all public services immediately and reckons the unemployed are unemployed because they don't want to work and that all migrants are potential terrorists, and every five years she begs me, with tears in her eyes, to get out and vote to save peace, freedom and democracy.

EVA: Well don't come crying to me.

LUCA: I'm all cried out, thanks.

EVA: Let's get together in three hours for the results. I don't want to be on my own.

She exits.

BARBARA: Luca?

LUCA: Yes.

BARBARA: What's your dream?

LUCA: To live through a real revolution. To be there at the birth of a fairer society. To see what it's like when there's enough energy to blow everything up. And to be young enough to be part of it. We talk about revolution, Barbara, the violence, the deaths, but we just don't realise what it was like. When I was a student, there was this old guy who lived in a tiny top-floor flat, an old-style revolutionary communist. I used to go round for tea and we'd talk for hours. The great workers' movements of the twentieth century, the revolutions betrayed, the hopes crushed. He'd been around at the start of the Cuban revolution. You just don't understand how it makes you feel, physically, he used to say. People are utterly changed, no longer ashamed of themselves. You feel as if you're in a brand-new body. He talked about the sheer thrill of mass freedom and all the changes it provokes artistically, poetically, emotionally, in every aspect of human relationships. So I'd like to be able to live through that one day, if I'm not too shrivelled up by bitterness. I'd like to feel a true community breaking out in freedom. You think I'm nuts? What's the matter? Why are you looking at me like that?

BARBARA leans in and kisses her. She breaks off.

BARBARA: I'm sorry. I shouldn't have done that. Sorry. I don't know what came over me.

LUCA: No harm done.

BARBARA: Revolution, yeah! I'm sorry. I'm not making fun. Things aren't great with Aymeric right now.

LUCA: Why are you with Aymeric, Barbara?

BARBARA: I don't know. But there's something inside me that does. And I don't understand it.

They sit on in the lobby of the theatre. We hear an ovation in the distance, shouts, and increasingly loud applause.

4.

Election night in the city. The Front Line party has won. Spontaneous demonstrations in the streets. Clashes.

JULIETTETE: They won!

AYMERIC: We have to stay calm.

JULIETTETE: Calm? We have an actual fascist as President! I'm not staying in this country.

AYMERIC: Everything will be fine.

JULIETTETE: I've had death threats.

AYMERIC: Just some nutter.

JULIETTETE: The white race.

AYMERIC: Let's see what happens.

JULIETTETE: Now they're in power?

AYMERIC: There'll be opposition.

JULIETTETE: I'm black.

AYMERIC: I know.

JULIETTETE: In a country that wants to defend the white race.

AYMERIC: We'll fight them from the inside.

JULIETTETE: Let's get out of here, Aymeric, let's go, let's change countries.

AYMERIC: We can't leave, we're the internal opposition.

JULIETTETE: I'm leaving Aymeric, come if you want but I'm leaving anyway.

AYMERIC: Don't do this Juliettete, stay, things are only just starting.

She's gone.

5.

Ovations. Shouting. Applause.

FABIEN MÜLLER: This is our country back, again and forever.

In spite of the struggles and the knives in the back.

Our one true nation once more and forever.

Applause.

This is my land

Here lie my ancestors and my long dead forebears

This is where I was born

To parents who were born right here themselves.

This is where I grew up

Where I've worked

Suffered

Loved

Here I stand on the soil of my native land

I'm proud of my roots

I'm not trying to interfere with other people's

But they'd better not come here and threaten mine

Applause.

You're afraid that your country's changing

Because you like it just the way it was

You're afraid of losing your land

Because you've spent your life here

Because you saw your children grow up here

And you've been mocked

And you've been blamed

And you've been looked down on

And you've been sneered at

Well let them sneer

Because today

You've won!

Howls of joy. Applause.

This victory is yours

The forgotten men and women

In the deep heart of our homeland

The honest, hardworking, silent masses

All of you who just didn't matter

Passed over again and again in favour of foreigners

You didn't ask for more

Than your work was worth

No, but no less either

You who knew how it burns to be humiliated

You who struggled against those who steal other people's jobs

For themselves

And all those who run the corrupt machinery of international capitalism

You the real people of the true country

You, my real people

You, my friends, who trusted and were betrayed

By those who were supposed to be on your side

All these metropolitan lefties who hate us

Because we tell the truth

You who love this country of ours

This great country

In all her power and timeless legend

You who take pride in your ancestors

You who are neither racist, xenophobic nor full of hate

Just because you don't understand why we should be building mosques

Where once were churches

All of you in the towns and the villages

The rolling shires and the countryside

Lost hamlets

Remote suburbia

You the real people

Who have carried us to power today

This victory is yours

We are the patriotic alternative

We are the Front Line

We are the real people

Who want our country back, again and forever

And we've won!

Wild applause. Shouts of joy.

6.

Lobby of the Balbek Theatre. AYMERIC has just arrived. NICOLE listens off to one side.

LUCA: Aymeric Dupré back in Balbek!

AYMERIC: Luca, my old friend, it's good to see you again.

LUCA: So you made it, you got famous.

AYMERIC: That's right.

LUCA: People talk about you.

AYMERIC: Not everyone.

LUCA: I'm happy for you, Aymeric.

AYMERIC: We can put on a new show now.

LUCA: One day maybe, not now though, I'm leaving.

AYMERIC: You're leaving?

LUCA: I've just resigned. The fascists are going to shut the theatre down. I was just getting my stuff.

AYMERIC: They're not going to close the theatre.

LUCA: That or give it to some brain-dead creep. Shall we have a drink?

AYMERIC: Where's Eva?

LUCA: At home. Total burnout. After all the shit these last few months.

AYMERIC: Luca, I need to tell you something.

LUCA: Shall we have a drink?

AYMERIC: I've been asked to take over as AD.

LUCA: By who?

AYMERIC: Fabien Müller.

LUCA: And?

AYMERIC: And I've accepted. I said yes. On condition that I can put on whatever I want. And that you work with me, Luca.

LUCA: You're going to work for them?

AYMERIC: I'm going to run a theatre.

LUCA: You're going to work for them.

AYMERIC: I will continue to defend art and culture.

LUCA: You're going to submit to these pigs.

AYMERIC: I'm going to keep this space safe.

LUCA: Living with them, negotiating with them.

AYMERIC: I want you to stay, Luca.

I want us to work together again.

A kind of internal resistance.

LUCA: There are spontaneous protests. Clashes every night in the streets. There are more and more of us. We're getting organised. I've got better things to do than resist from the inside.

AYMERIC: Being director of this theatre, I can be useful.

LUCA: Useful to who? I'm leaving.

AYMERIC: Useful to people, Luca.

To the ordinary people of Balbek.

Young people with no access to culture.

To us!

LUCA: Can you please let go of my arm?

AYMERIC: I've got where I am by my own efforts. I worked hard to get to where I am today. And now you want me to leave? Because the people of my country have made a choice which I'm not totally thrilled about? Who am I to tell them they're wrong? Who am I to know what's right? To tell others what to do or think? I'm just an actor. The Front Line were elected in a democratic vote. I accept the results. I'm a democrat.

LUCA: Aymeric, please let go of my arm.

He lets go.

LUCA: How the hell did we get here?

He exits.

NICOLE: I don't understand why you need him.

AYMERIC: You think I'm a scumbag, don't you?

NICOLE: Not at all. You have to be pragmatic. And Luca never was.

AYMERIC: He's always been over the top. A caricature. But he's a good person. Sweet. Terribly sweet. A gentle revolutionary.

NICOLE: And what's the first play you're going to do here?

AYMERIC: *Hamlet.*

NICOLE: And would you have a part for me, Mr Director?

AYMERIC: Ophelia?

7.

Balbek. Night. Outside. The little church is on fire. Sound of disturbances in the distance. MICHAEL carries a can of petrol.

LUCA: Who started the fire?

MICHAEL: Muslims.

LUCA: Michael, are you all right?

MICHAEL: Don't patronise me.

LUCA: Your mother.

MICHAEL: I FORBID YOU TO TALK TO MY MOTHER.

LUCA: She told me you're not doing too great.

MICHAEL: I'm not mad.

LUCA: Who started the fire?

MICHAEL: The fucking Muslims. The terrorists. We need a war, a bloody great war. This has all gone on long enough;

we need things back in place. We need to purify the world. We have to kill the terrorists, we have to clear out the Muslims, we have to defend ourselves. We have to defend Europe. The real Europe. Our country. Our real country

LUCA: Michael, this is rubbish.

MICHAEL: STOP CONTRADICTING ME.

LUCA: Come with me.

MICHAEL: Let me go, please. I'll pretend I didn't see you or I'll say you're one of us. Go home, Luca. FUCK OFF! FUCK OFF! DO YOU UNDERSTAND? FUCK OFF OUT OF HERE OR I'LL KILL YOU!

LUCA: Your leader, Fabien Müller, has asked Aymeric to take over the theatre. He didn't offer it to you, Michael. He didn't offer it to one of your people. You play at being the great white warriors, you're fools, you'll be crushed.

MICHAEL: Fuck the theatre. FUCK OFF.

LUCA: Go home.

MICHAEL: FUCK OFF.

LUCA: Think about your mother.

MICHAEL: FUCK OFF, LUCA! FUCK OFF! LET ME THROUGH.

MICHAEL and LUCA shove each other. Then MICHAEL takes out a gun and, maybe accidentally, maybe not, shoots LUCA, who falls. LUCA doesn't move.

Night. In the distance the church burns.

PART SIX

ELSINORE

1.

Chorus of the newly exiled.

It always starts with a little detail

A nothing

That no one notices at first

A crumbling wall

A crack in a window pane

And no one pays attention

Someone who used to laugh all the time

Suddenly going quiet

And we used to look at the city

And its avenues in the evening time

Wide open avenues like veins

In the translucent lights

All seemed so modern

More than modern

Suddenly becoming obsolete

Stupid

Sterile

Sagging

We watched things getting worse.

Getting dirty

Children's playgrounds haunted by armed shadows
at night

Dust

Herds of lonely men in bars all day

Those first houses set on fire deliberately

For the insurance

Seals on doors

Evictions

And the agony of starting to lose

Lose everything

And the acceptance

So we had to leave

And the city slowly emptied itself

The first departures

Friends talking weird stuff

Or waking up at night

Or sleeping outside

In the Northern Southern Eastern Western districts

In the central districts

Near cinemas or tube exits

In the neighbourhoods

Where nothing worked anymore but the sky

Always the same as before

Wide

Ample

Inaccessible

And the great call of elsewhere

And the sea

Of some other life starting over again elsewhere

In another city

In other crowds with other people

And other reflexes and other music

And other bodies

Other morning lights in other mornings and other morning songs

And different people in your daily life

Different kitchens programs windows partitions

Streets and avenues

Different faces

Far from the groans

Far from the wreckage of here

And the complaints from here.

And from the land

And the hunger here

And the dreams here

And the terrible deathly boredom of here

And low-key suicides in the flats right here

Two blocks from here

And the crisis here

And the fascism here

And the bitter legends of old Europe

2.

Evening. The stage of the Balbek Theatre. AYMERIC addresses a pig's head.

AYMERIC: 'Angels and ministers of grace defend us!
    Be thou a spirit of health or goblin damn'd,
    Bring with thee airs from heaven or blasts from hell,
    Be thy intents wicked or charitable,
    Thou com'st in such a questionable shape
    That I will speak to thee. What may this mean
    That thou, dead corse, again in complete steel,
    Revisits thus the glimpses of the moon,
    Making night hideous, and we fools of nature
    So horridly to shake our disposition
    With thoughts beyond the reaches of our souls?
    Say, why is this? wherefore? What should we do?'

Enter MICHAEL as Horatio

AYMERIC: 'Who art thou?'

MICHAEL: 'Horatio'

AYMERIC: 'What would'st thou, Horatio?'

MICHAEL: 'Help you revenge your father'

AYMERIC: 'My father has been dead for years'

Silence.

AYMERIC: Line?

MICHAEL: 'He was an alcoholic slave'

AYMERIC: 'My father has been dead for years. He was an alcoholic slave'

Silence.

AYMERIC: Line?

MICHAEL: 'He lived by a pig farm. In a rural part of the Kingdom. He wasn't the King of Denmark'

AYMERIC: 'My father has been dead for years, Horatio. He was an alcoholic slave. He lived by a pig farm. In a distant rural part of the Kingdom. He wasn't the King of Denmark'

MICHAEL: 'I knew your father well'

AYMERIC: 'He drank to drown his shame at what he was. A slave to the King of Denmark. And he made me drink too'

MICHAEL: 'He made you drink, Hamlet, and curse the entire world. And the King of Denmark. And your sister drank too so that the bottle would be over quicker. And you were always afraid that, once the bottle was done, he'd open another'

Silence.

AYMERIC: Line?

MICHAEL: 'How do you know all this, Horatio?'

AYMERIC: 'How do you know all this, Horatio? How do you know the story of Hamlet so well?'

MICHAEL: 'Everyone knows the story of Hamlet. Here in Denmark's royal piggery. For it is not only your father's story but the story of all our fathers. Small businessmen, small shopkeepers, workmen, craftsmen. It's the story of all the King of Denmark's slaves. I shall help you kill your father's murderer'

AYMERIC: 'Who killed my father? Speak Horatio! Tell me all'

MICHAEL: 'The King of Denmark'

AYMERIC: 'I was always told my father died of a heart attack brought on by alcoholism'

MICHAEL: 'The King of Denmark was responsible for his long decline and for his death. Follow me'

AYMERIC: 'Where are we now, Horatio? It's so gloomy'

MICHAEL: 'Elsinore'

AYMERIC: 'I can't see. Lead me on. Take me to the King of Denmark. I'll cut his throat and take his head back and throw it in amongst the pigs with all the others. My father shall be revenged'

They exit. Blackout.

3.

And Aymeric's alone now

In the dark

And he walks

And shadows quiver on the walls

AYMERIC: Is anyone there?

And suddenly Aymeric

Has no idea where he is

And something cracks

AYMERIC: Is anyone there?

He walks

Outside

It's night

On the desolate plain

AYMERIC: Is there anyone there?

Churches finish burning in the night

Men trudge home

With bloodied sacks on their backs

AYMERIC: Is anyone there?

THE MAJORDOMO: I'm so sorry, I didn't hear you come in!
Come on, you're late, the party's already started.

AYMERIC: I'm looking for the King of Denmark

THE MAJORDOMO: Come on in

And the gate swings open

And the butler leads Aymeric

Into the great house

To a vast dining-room

Where he sees men drinking blood from glasses

That never seem to empty

AYMERIC: That's weird, you drink and drink but your glass is always full?

THE BUTLER: The blood never runs out. The blood of humankind is infinite. And our glasses never run dry. Fascism is a fabulous show that gets revived from time to time to shake things up and let everyone escape for a while from the tedium of ordinary life and the crushing boredom of democracy. So welcome. I'll take you to the artists' table.

And the butler takes Aymeric by the arm

and leads him to a table

At the back of the room

THE BUTLER: May I introduce Richard Strauss, composer and conductor?

KLAUS MANN: Did very well under the Nazis.

THE BUTLER: Wilhelm Furtwängler, composer and conductor.

KLAUS MANN: Did very well under the Nazis.

THE BUTLER: Gottfried Benn, expressionist poet.

KLAUS MANN: Hung around and did very well under the Nazis.

THE BUTLER: And Klaus Mann, a rubbish hack.

KLAUS MANN: You couldn't spare ten euros, could you?

RICHARD STRAUSS: Oh, give over, Klaus.

AYMERIC: I think I'm at the wrong table.

THE BUTLER: No, no. This is the right one.

WILHELM FURTWÄNGLER: This is the artists' table, look, here's your name-card.

RICHARD STRAUSS: You're..?

AYMERIC: Aymeric Dupré.

RICHARD STRAUSS: That's right then. Look.

KLAUS MANN: You wouldn't have ten euros, would you?

RICHARD STRAUSS: Oh do go away, Klaus

WILHELM FURTWÄNGLER: We've told you a hundred times. Clear off!

GOTTFRIED BENN: You don't belong here.

AYMERIC: Who is he?

KLAUS MANN: Klaus Mann.

AYMERIC: Never heard of him.

KLAUS MANN: Mephisto?

AYMERIC: No, means nothing.

KLAUS MANN: Have you never read Faust?

RICHARD STRAUSS: Don't speak to him, my dear Aymeric, he's an addict, he just wants money for morphine.

GOTTFRIED BENN: There's a dealer outside under the Arch, we can't get rid of him.

RICHARD STRAUSS: He'll just score his gear and shoot up in a corner.

WILHELM FURTWÄNGLER: I don't know why he's been foisted on us.

RICHARD STRAUSS: We can't seem to get rid of him.

GOTTFRIED BENN: He's a failed writer.

RICHARD STRAUSS: He doesn't have his father's talent.

KLAUS MANN: My father used to say I wrote too fast. Well he wrote too slowly; for a time long gone when you could hunker down behind solid bourgeois walls like these and spend days at a time just reading. I wrote this novel. I've written in it for you.

AYMERIC: I'm not interested.

KLAUS MANN: To my dear Hendrik Höfgen, with sadness, disappointment and, frankly, puzzlement. Klaus Mann.

AYMERIC: I'm not Hendrik Höfgen. You're getting me mixed up with someone else.

KLAUS MANN: We get people mixed up. We get the times mixed up. Of course we do. I was inspired to write it by an old friend who's very like you. You wouldn't have ten euros, would you?

AYMERIC: I don't have any money.

KLAUS MANN: You're rolling in it. Like Strauss. Like Furtwängler. Like Gottfried. Like everyone who makes a deal with authority.

GOTTFRIED BENN: I'm a dermatologist, Klaus, I've spent my life examining and treating the genitals of prostitutes. It didn't make me rich.

KLAUS MANN: Give us ten euros.

RICHARD STRAUSS: Get him out of here.

WILHELM FURTWÄNGLER: Can someone call security?

GOTTFRIED BENN: Get out of here, Klaus.

RICHARD STRAUSS: I can't bear drug addicts.

THE BUTLER: Here, Mr Mann, sir, here's your fix, if you could please keep your voice down.

WILHELM FURTWÄNGLER: I come out to the country for a bit of peace. I read. I compose. I play Beethoven. If you only knew how many years of work it takes to play a single bar of Beethoven as it should be played; years of concentration. It doesn't matter who's listening to the music we play. It's not my problem who's in the audience. I PLAY BEETHOVEN. I don't have time for anything else. And this drugged-up journalist comes pestering us.

And, listening to Furtwängler

Drinking toasts with Richard Strauss

Laughing with Gottfried Benn

Aymeric Dupré feels reassured

And my brother, Klaus Mann, injects himself with morphine

Slumped in his chair

Drooling into his plate

RICHARD STRAUSS: KLAUS YOU'RE DISGUSTING!

Aymeric Dupré is at peace

Strangely enough

He is finally rid of the weight of Balbek

And the little throbbing guilt he feels about the theatre people there

Because you can hate yourself when you're a failure

But not when you're winning

AYMERIC: I think I'm in the wrong period.

WILHELM FURTWÄNGLER: No, no, Dupré, that's your name all right.

RICHARD STRAUSS: You're at the 'great artists' table and you're most welcome.

KLAUS MANN: They're not all here, some of them left, some of them refused to stay!

GOTTFRIED BENN: Oh shut up, Mann!

RICHARD STRAUSS: What can I get you, Aymeric?

AYMERIC: OK. I'll have a glass of red wine, I think.

And as they pour a glass for Aymeric

My brother shudders

And the morphine floods

Into his veins

And he stands

Knocking over the tables

RICHARD STRAUSS: God, he's so boring.

WILHELM FURTWÄNGLER: Can someone call security?

4.

May 1949, a hotel room in Cannes. KLAUS MANN slumped on a bed.
His sister ERIKA appears as if in a dream.

ERIKA: Klaus? Klaus? Klaus, it's me. It's Erika. Your sister. What are you doing?

KLAUS: I'm leaving, Erika.

ERIKA: Where Klaus? Where are you going?

KLAUS: Death.

ERIKA: Why are you doing this, Klaus? Why are you dying?

KLAUS: I am so alone, so hopelessly alone.

ERIKA: Klaus, it's me, it's us, I'm here.

KLAUS: Where are we?

ERIKA: In your hotel room, Klaus. In Cannes. This is the room where you're going to kill yourself ten minutes from now, Klaus, my love. I don't want you to kill yourself, Klaus. Why don't you wait till tomorrow? The day after tomorrow? The day after that? What if we still have things to live for?

KLAUS: Everything's been destroyed, Erika.

ERIKA: Klaus, please, stay.

KLAUS: I had this dream, Erika. I dreamt of a man who lies yet never lies. And who wins every time. And who always gets away with it. And it starts all over again and again. Over and over again. In the dream it all started all over again. Everything started all over again. The same characters on the same stage. And in the dream, I was

rewriting *Mephisto*. It's always this novel. I have to rewrite
it every time, again, again, and again, and one more time
again. Always the same and always different. Always
the same scenes, just like before but different. Like a
rhapsody. And it gets turned down every time, Erika. The
publishers turn it down every time. And I was alone. And
we were alone, Erika. And our struggle. And our struggles.
I'm so tired. Erika. So tired. My sister. My love. So tired.

ERIKA: I'm right here, Klaus. I'm here with you.

Suicide.